Scared Great

Dedication

To my wife Jessica and my children
Kendra Jae, Famous Kobe J and Kaleb J

*"It's not about how big you can dream, it's about
how long you can dream big."*

I live to love my family.

Acknowledgements

One of my biggest fears that kept me from completing this Scared Great book project was the thought of having to do it by myself. That one thought paralyzed my progress for years. I would be remiss to expect you to continue reading without acknowledging those who read, made suggestions, gave feedback, edited etc. Scared Great to its completion.

Jessica Bracy aka Mrs. Make it Happen, Susan Schultz aka Coach Kindness, Suzie Cohen, John Kohls, Sam and Judi Cohen, Les Brown, Tami Fandrei, Lisa Sullivan, Leesa Fowler, Laura Jenkins, Heather Kelley, Susan Anderson, Hillary Hartwell, Lisa Catlett, Kari Butler, Tyler Forge and Ingrid Carson.

Thank you for taking the time to help me turn an extremely rough, rough draft of stories, ideas and life lessons into something that I could be proud of and excited to share with the world.

I appreciate each and every one of you. I could not have done this without you.

KB

Scared Great

"This book is intended for people who experience the normal fears associated with making major life changes. If you are experiencing anxiety that is so pervasive and intense that it interferes with major life functions like working or engaging in normal day-to-day activities, please seek professional help. Very effective techniques are available for people with debilitating anxiety."

Foreword
By Les Brown

Kevin Bracy, great husband, proud father, dynamic speaker and trainer has written a groundbreaking book for people who have goals and dreams but have allowed their fears to stop them. We are all born with only two fears -- the fear of falling and the fear of loud noises; all the rest of our fears are manufactured in our minds. Kevin has opened the avenue of another kind of fear – he calls it Scared Great.

That title speaks to me. The fear of not being remembered, the fear of not using all the talents and abilities I have been given has haunted me for a very long time. I believe that we were created on purpose with a purpose for a purpose and Kevin has truly tapped into that. He speaks to those of us who really feel that, if we had our lives to live over again, we could have done more. Kevin is using the idea of fear -- of being scared -- to motivate and inspire us and to challenge us to live life with a sense of urgency, to give our best at all times under all circumstances, and to take no prisoners and treat the wounded.

That's who Kevin is and that's what people love about him. Not only is he the messenger, but he is also the message. Kevin speaks to us through his love, his insight and his passion. Kevin and the whole team he has put together are committed to helping young people, educators, teachers and parents come together to lead, guide and facilitate children becoming assets to our society and the world.

When Kevin speaks and when young people and adults go through his trainings, transformative experiences occur. Kevin helps give people a larger vision of themselves. He touches their hearts, ignites their spirits, and empowers them to become what Mother Teresa would call "Pencils in the hand of God to begin writing new chapters in their lives." This book is a guide to that kind of empowerment.

Kevin has a true gift. He has the ability to look beyond the behaviors, attitudes, and disruptive and dysfunctional habits many of us embrace and stimulate us to begin to pursue our greatness. Kevin helps us realize we can broaden our lives to give all we have; he helps us 'release our imprisoned splendor' and become catalysts of action and the embodiment of hope. Kevin helps us understand that having hope for the future gives us power in the present; it gives us the ability to control our own destiny. This book is a blueprint written with that in mind.

As he helps us to change what we see in ourselves and what we say to ourselves, Kevin encourages us to pull out and tap into the unlimited potential each of us has and to express it. He's inspiring us to become risk takers in order to become our best selves. It has been said that: "If you're not willing to risk, you can't grow. If you can't grow, you can't become your best, and if you can't become your best, you can't be happy. If you can't be happy, then what else is there?"

Scared Great is about living a life of no regrets, one in which you 'live full and die empty,' as Dr. Miles Monroe once said. This book asks, "What do you want to do with your life?" It asks us to think about where we are now and how we see ourselves five years from now, 10 years from now. It encourages us to use our fear to push ourselves forward, to challenge ourselves, to break through just living and begin to take life on.

Kevin believes we all have so much to share, so much to give. He has written this book to help us see that our fears don't have to paralyze us. They can push us forward, enable us to break through the walls of mediocrity and create a strong sense within ourselves that we're just not comfortable living a small life.

In this book Scared Great, he has given us ways to operationalize the thinking of Henry David Thoreau, who said, "If a man does not keep pace with his companions, perhaps he's listening to the beat of a different drummer. Let him dance to the music he hears however, measured or far apart."

Scared Great is a handbook for living a life with no regrets, on the cutting edge, doing all you can, where you are with what you have. Helen Keller said, "Life is either a daring adventure or nothing at all." Scared Great is a guide to living each of our own 'daring adventures.' It teaches us to embrace our fear and move forward anyhow.

I found each chapter touching in a special way and expect that each reader may well have a similar experience. I encourage you, the reader, to take time with family members, friends and coworkers, perhaps develop a study group, to go through each chapter thoroughly in order to make the most of Kevin's detailed and methodical approach to becoming Scared Great.

I'm so proud of you, Kevin. You've done me proud.

Thank you for sharing your greatness with us all.

That's my story and I'm sticking to it.

Les Brown

TABLE OF CONTENTS

SCARED GREAT

HOW I GOT THE TITLE FOR THIS BOOK

Recently, I was having a Q&A session with a group of administrators and educators at a community day school in Lodi, California. These difference-makers were brainstorming about which parts of our Reach One Program (our bully prevention and character-building program) they wanted us to implement on their campus. Whenever I'm in these types of meetings I like to have my assistant coach, Susan Schultz, aka Coach Kindness, with me because she thrives and shines and helps enormously in these brainstorming environments. When Susan and I go onto a school campus, we have superhero names. Her superhero name is Coach Kindness because she is compassionate, she has an amazing way of connecting with people and communities through her kindness. I'm Coach Greatness, not because I'm so great, but because I see the greatness in people.

On this particular day, I was in the front of the room talking to the group, when Susan spoke up from the back of the room. She said, "We've got to get your students in front of Kevin multiple times throughout the year so he can establish a connection with them because he has the ability to help them see their greatness. I know your kids are scared of what their futures might hold, scared that they can't make it. What Kevin is going to do is *scare them Great*."

I thought, *That's it! That's what I've been doing all these years.* I've been scaring myself into Greatness. And that's the message I'm trying to share with the kids I work with.

I had never put those words to it. After the brainstorming session adjourned and Susan and I had gone our separate ways, I sat in my car for several minutes, just thinking about what she said, "scare them Great." I thought about the fact that even though I've been doing this work for many years now, it's always the same. Every time I'm about to go on stage or get in front of a group to present, I'm *scared.* Every time I finish a talk or a presentation, if I can look in the mirror and know I gave it my best, I feel *great.*

That moment in the mirror is my measure of Greatness. I ask myself: Did I prepare enough? Did I channel those butterflies in my belly into something useful that other people could hear and understand? Did I give it my best focus, best preparation, best effort? Did I show up as the best version of myself? If I can say "yes" to myself in that moment, then I know I've achieved my definition of Greatness.

It doesn't matter how scared I felt beforehand.

Being scared is part of the process.
Being scared is being human.

Susan was absolutely right. I had been living in a state of fear for as long as I could remember, scared I wouldn't live to see age 20, scared I wasn't smart enough in school, handsome enough to ever find a wife, talented enough in baseball, scared I was going to be average in my life, scared I'd never make it as a professional speaker. Although I didn't know it, I was *'scaring myself* into Greatness' all this time.

After the presentation, I had to call Susan from my car and tell her, "Thank you! You gave me the title for my book. I have been thinking about and vacillating over a book title for years. What you said in that meeting resonated with my spirit and it fits my life like a custom suit. 'Scared Great' is going to be the name of my book!"

Every time I walk into a classroom, gymnasium, hotel ballroom, corporate board room and/or event center to speak I know that every human being has Greatness within them. I know that 100 percent. I do not doubt that for a moment; it's woven into the fabric of my belief system. I also know the people I'll be talking to have *fear and* I know that fear doesn't just magically disappear when one hears a few motivational words. The truth is, the fear is the beginning, the *source* of personal Greatness.

INTRODUCTION

It's Oct 18, 2015. I've just boarded a plane in Chicago after giving a speech for the March of Dimes. Next stop — Burbank, California, where I'll be shooting a live broadcast for the National Society of Leadership and Success.

As I buckle myself into seat 3B, I think, "Brace yourself, Bracy." Mentally, I'm preparing myself for the upcoming broadcast by rehearsing my opening lines in my head. It's just like putting on my seatbelt to prepare for takeoff.

On the broadcast, I'll be interviewing the legendary leader, John C. Maxwell, who has inspired millions of people all over the world with his best-selling books and inspirational speeches. This man is the maven of leadership development; I'm grateful for this opportunity to speak with him.

Sometimes I still can't believe where this journey has taken me. I remember a time when the idea of speaking for two minutes at a Toastmasters meeting almost sent me into a panic. Yet, for the last 22 years, I've been living my dream of being a professional speaker. I've presented all over the United States, and even had the opportunity to speak outside the US while traveling with the legendary icon of motivational speaking, Les Brown.

I don't want to do anything else with my life other than this. I feel blessed to be able to do what I love every day. What do I love about this work? Connecting with people from all walks of life, hearing their stories, expressing the belief I have in others and using my words to inspire them. I sincerely believe that everyone has Greatness within themselves and I love using my gift of communication to help them draw it out.

You would think that after all these years of presenting to thousands of students, teachers and administrators, parents, student athletes and corporate professionals, I'd get to a point where I'd have no more fear about speaking in public.

Yet, as the plane taxis down the runway, I notice that I am feeling 'some kinda way' in my bosom. I dial into the feeling and realize *I'm scared*. Is it because I haven't rehearsed? No way. I'll be using a script that I've delivered thousands of times in my private rehearsals. I know confidence comes from preparation, and I rehearse my speeches like Peyton Manning studied defenses.

But even with all that practice, I'm uneasy. I'm nervous. I'm scared to mess it up.

My *scared* stems from the fact that the show depends on me. I know the organization is counting on me to represent leadership and success in the powerful way that their brand is accustomed to. I'm scared because what I'm about to do matters, and I know it matters.

So, yes, I'm scared about this broadcast. But that doesn't mean being scared is a bad thing. It isn't something I have to run from. Instead, I'm taking it as a sign that I need to prepare more. I have a few hours on this flight to go over my script, get in a few more repetitions, and diminish that fear as much as possible. At the same time, I know the fear won't go away completely — and I realize I don't want it to.

When faced with a challenge, there is nothing more normal than feeling fear. There's nothing wrong with fear. Fear is an indicator that what we are doing is important. It's an opportunity to step into our Greatness. We can be *scared*, and still be great anyway.

Without being *scared*, maybe I don't prepare as much, leading to a totally different result. Without being *scared*, maybe I don't give 100 percent of my Best Effort, Best Focus, Best Version of Me, using my Best Talent.

Too often, people let fear drive them away from their Greatness. Fear can stop people from pursuing their dreams. Fear can make people run away from challenges instead of tackling them. I know because I have done it myself.

Most of us have heard over and over again that we need to 'get over' our fears or 'work around' them. But today, as I sit here with this fear, I'm realizing there is another way to look at it. Instead of trying to ignore my fear or overcome it, I can use it.

I can steer my fear, instead of allowing it to steer me.

Starting Out Scared

My earliest memories are of being scared. I remember long nights when my brother Derrick and I were very young, and we'd been left alone in our duplex in Sacramento. My dad was a drummer, and when he went out gigging on the weekends my mom would often go with him. My brother and I would be left without any adults to make us feel safe; it seemed like those nights went on forever.

The fear would start to grip us as soon as we saw our parents getting dressed to go out. We knew there would be drinking, maybe drugs too. We knew whenever drinking was part of the equation it always — and I mean always — turned out negatively. My dad was unpredictable when he drank, and he often lashed out at my mom and us. We didn't know how intense the arguing or violence might be when they came home, and we feared that unknown.

We'd watch our parents through the window as they backed the burgundy Camaro out of the driveway. Then the fear of being left all alone at night would start to creep in. Derrick and I would huddle together on the side of the couch away from the window, where we felt we couldn't be seen or heard. For hours, we'd watch TV from our little bubble, only getting up when we had to go to the bathroom or get something to eat. And even then, we'd run as fast as we could to get back to our safe spot.

We'd watch TV for 3, 4, 5, 6, hours until it was midnight and there was nothing left to watch in those days. Then we'd look at the stained-glass window near the front door, where we could see the headlights of passing cars. Each time the lights would shine through the window, we'd get excited that our parents might be home, and then be disappointed when the lights didn't make the turn into the driveway. We'd be so tired, but too afraid to close our eyes and fall asleep because we didn't know what we'd wake up to.

When the headlights finally made that turn into the driveway and we knew our parents were home, the fear would go away for one second. At least we weren't alone anymore. But as we watched our parents' shadows cross the window and heard the key in the lock, the fear would come right back. Now we were scared about what would happen next. Would there be fighting? How long would it last? How loud would it be? Will I have to walk a mile to the payphone in the dark with my mom because we had to get out due to the intensity of the fight, AGAIN?

Those nights were no fun at all. I'm glad that type of fear is over. I want never to live through it again. At the same time, I wouldn't go back in time and change anything if I had the chance, because it's all a part of who I am now. For one thing, my experience taught me a lot about what *not* to do as I raise my own kids.

In the fearful environment of my childhood, I latched onto a dream — to play professional baseball. Of course, I wanted my life and my future to be different from how I'd grown up, and I saw baseball as the way to make that happen. On top of that, I genuinely loved playing because it gave me a feeling of accomplishment and confidence. I lived and breathed baseball, from age nine, all the way through my twenties. There were a lot of disappointments in store for me. There were times when my lack of inner confidence got the best of me. There were times I turned away from challenges. There were times when I let that voice of fear get to me.

But there were also the moments when I got the right message from a friend, coach, teacher or mentor and decided not to give up. There were the moments when I trusted myself and followed my instincts. There were times when I believed in myself enough to keep working and keep practicing even though it wasn't easy. And there were a lot of times when I managed to talk myself into Greatness, even though there was a different script playing in my head.

I know there are a lot of kids out there who have to deal with being scared at home, like I did. There are also many adults out there who remember being scared as a kid. No matter what our life experiences have been, I know that every single one of us has felt afraid at one time or another. I also know that every single one of us has Greatness within us; we can show up and be great every single day.

Fear is normal. It's nothing to be ashamed of. We don't have to run from it or let it drive us in the wrong direction. We can approach it, recognize it, breathe through it, and steer it. Every one of us can steer our fear towards Greatness.

When you do, you'll be absolutely floored by all you can accomplish and how many others you can reach with your Greatness.

Did I get over being scared? Did I stop having the *feeling* of scared? Twenty-two years and thousands of speeches later, NO. I'm still scared. If something matters, I'm scared. I've just learned to steer my fear towards Greatness, my *own* Greatness, not anybody else's definition of it.

I believe we all have access to Greatness, every single person on this earth. And every day is another chance we're given to live from that Greatness. That doesn't mean we ever stop feeling the *scared*. There's no magic trick to make that go away — and there shouldn't be. Feeling scared means we have an opportunity to step into our Greatness.

So, brace yourself to steer your fear toward your Greatness.

CHAPTER ONE: DON'T COME BACK WITHOUT YOUR SHOES

When I was growing up in Citrus Heights, California, during basketball season the fellas around the neighborhood would play some competitive games on the weekends — basketball during basketball season, football during football season, baseball during baseball season etc. ....

One weekend I was shooting hoops outside my friend Pat Robinson's house. He was three years older than I was, and a whole lot bigger. The only trouble with those highly competitive neighborhood games was how quickly things could get 'chippy,' i.e. aggressively belligerent. All it would take is for someone to get elbowed, or someone's teen angst to get fired up. Before you knew it, you were looking at a knock-down fist fight.

I was twelve years old when I got dragged into one of those fights and I'll never forget it. I wasn't looking for it, but I walked away from that Sunday afternoon with an important life lesson.

I don't remember what it was that set Pat off. All I remember is the force he used to slam the ball into me as he squared up to fight. As a younger brother, I was no stranger to 'knuckling up.' Even though the odds were against me, the only thing I could do was man up. The fight was on.

Pat launched an uppercut that hit me right below my sternum. The punch dropped me to my knees. I had never had the wind knocked out of me like that. I was like a fish out of water, powerless and gasping for breath.

I crouched on the ground with both arms wrapped around myself, desperate to get a lungful of air. I knew I was defeated. I felt like I was about to die. I looked up at Pat, wondering if he was going to throw another punch. He reached down.

For one sweet moment, I thought he was going to offer a hand to help me up. Instead, he pulled the white velcro Stadia's off my feet. Then he pitched them over the fence into his yard, where his two dogs lived.

Everyone on my street — and probably in the city of Citrus Heights — knew I was afraid of dogs.

Those shoes were as good as gone. There was no way I was going after them to get eaten alive by those two yappy beagle dogs of his. I managed to get to my feet, still gasping for air, and started limping down the block back to my own house. I looked over my shoulder to see Pat's father watching from the back yard. He had seen the whole fight and said nothing. I had never felt so helpless.

I walked into my house, hunched over and defeated. My dad was in the kitchen ironing his clothes for work the next day. As soon as he saw me, he asked, "Where are your shoes, boy?"

I could barely speak. With tears running down my face, I gasped out the words, "Pat punched me in my...my...my...stomach. He took...my shoes off my feet and...and threw them over the fence."

My dad slammed the iron down on the ironing board and said, "Getcho ass out of my house and go getcho mutha-fuckin shoes back! What the hell is wrong with you? You think to let someone take yo shoes off yo god damn feet and throw them over a fence, and then come back in my house in yo socks?"

The humiliation started to sink in. I hadn't even *tried* to get my shoes back. I had been a coward, and my dad wasn't going to let me get away with it.

I gathered myself with a quick drink of Kool-Aid as he continued yelling. "...you bet not ever in your life come back in my house with no shoes on yo feet! Get yo ass outside and don't come back without yo shoes."

I walked back out the front door. I stood there on the porch step for a minute, shoeless, shaking, and with my dad still cussing at me from the kitchen. I knew I had a decision to make.

My options:
1. Go back in the house and defy my father;
2. Go back out and fight this older kid who had just taken not only my breath but my spirit as well;
3. Go back over the fence, grab my shoes, and get eaten alive by those dogs.

Every single one of my options filled me with fear. There wasn't any easy way out.

I had to steer my fear into something useful. I channeled it all into one big, deep breath. I wiped the tears off my face, squared my shoulders, and found my pride. Then, I swaggered back down the street with the confidence of a kid twice my size.

Pat was still shooting baskets. As I walked up, his shot hit the rim and the ball came bouncing toward me. I grabbed the ball and dropkicked it all the way down the street, challenging him with every step I took. I put my knuckles up and we got into fight number two.

Bracy vs. Robinson Rematch

There was no way I was leaving without my shoes this time. All the pain, humiliation and fear I felt came out of my fists as punches. I didn't think about the fact that Pat was bigger than me. I didn't think about the dogs barking like crazy on the other side of the fence. This time, the fight ended with me taking Patrick's shoes off *his* feet and throwing them over the fence. Now that he was defeated, Pat had to go into his yard and throw my shoes back to me.

I was victorious! I could go home and face my dad without shame. I could look in the mirror without shame. I had channeled my fear into winning a fight I had no business winning that day.

I want to make it clear that I am NOT an advocate of violence. I don't think it's a good way to solve problems and I definitely avoid it; however, on that day I did what I had to do. If I hadn't gone back to Pat's house and faced my fear, this guy would have taken my spirit every time I saw him. My dad *knew* that, which is what made him a great leader that Sunday afternoon.

What my dad taught me that day wasn't about throwing punches, and it wasn't about shoes, either. What he taught me was: 'Have pride in who you are. Don't you ever let someone take the shoes off your feet.'

Life itself will take the shoes off your feet if you let it. Life will take *all* your stuff if you let it. And life isn't going anywhere. It's always going to be filled with obstacles and challenges; we can't predict what those will be. That's a constant.

What are you going to do when faced with those challenges? That's the real question. And that's where you have the power to choose.

If I had passively walked away and let those dogs eat my shoes, what then? How many more pairs of shoes would I allow to get taken off my feet? How many dreams would I give up because of fear? How many chances for Greatness in my life would I hand away if I allow fear to make my decisions for me?

What if, instead, I learn to embrace that fear? What if I channel that fear? Then it becomes a *directed* force. It becomes an asset and strength in my life.

The fear you feel is useful. It doesn't have to defeat you. You can use that fear to turn the tables and win *the day*.

CHAPTER TWO: FROM 'SCARED STRAIGHT' TO 'SCARED GREAT'

Back in the 70s, my parents made us sit down and watch a movie called *Scared Straight*. It was a documentary in which at-risk kids — 'juvenile delinquents,' as they were called — were exposed to inmates in the prison system. The idea was simple: scare the kids into not doing crime. These young people were taken to a state prison and basically yelled at for hours by inmates who were serving life sentences. The inmates were terrifying, and they did their best to scare the kids into being 'straight.'

Since that documentary was made, only one of the original group of kids ended up in jail. But when the same idea was used by a series of TV shows, the results weren't as successful. In fact, it has been argued that this tactic makes the problem worse in some cases.

I was pretty scared by that movie when I saw it as a kid. But the truth is, I was scared all the time anyway. My home life was unstable and scary most of the time. My parents fought a lot; I have more memories than I can count of my dad being intoxicated and doing the most unpredictable things. By way of example, I vividly recall the night he almost set my grandmother's house on fire because she wouldn't give him five dollars.

I was a teenager at the time. I was talking with my friend, Holly, in the living room at my grandparents' house — Big Mama and Gramps, we called them. As soon as my dad walked into the house, the fear rose up in my chest. I could tell he had been drinking. He said barely a word to us, just walked straight back to Big Mama's room where she was sleeping. For some reason, he was carrying a gas can. Pretty soon, Holly and I heard their voices rising in an argument.

"I need five dollars for gas," my dad was saying.

"John, I don't even have five dollars right now," said Big Mama. "I don't have any money."

My dad kept demanding money, his voice getting louder and louder. Holly and I sat there for a few minutes, feeling more and more uncomfortable. Finally, I knew I had to do something. I walked back into Big Mama's room and tried to intervene.

"Dad, come on," I said. "Big Mama doesn't have any money right now. Can't you just let her go back to sleep?"

My dad turned on me instantly. "Oh, you think you're big enough to whoop me now?" he yelled, swinging the gas can around wildly as he turned in my direction.

"No, Dad, I'm not trying to fight you; I'm just saying Big Mama doesn't have any money right now." I was trying desperately to calm him down, but I knew it was useless. Once he was in this kind of mood, things were only going to escalate.

He pushed past me, walking back into the middle room of the house, between the living room and bedrooms. He was slinging the gas can around like he was going to spill it, and then he pulled out a lighter. "You wanna fight me?" he demanded, holding the lighter up in one hand, and the gas can in the other. "You think you bad enough? Come on! I will blow this motherfucka up!"

He's gonna kill all of us, I thought. I rushed at him and tried to grab the gas can. As I wrestled with him, he fell backwards. The top of the can popped off and he flung it towards me.

Gasoline came gushing out, hitting me in the face and drenching me. It was like being under water. I couldn't breathe, see, or hear. Blindly, I started punching. Years of accumulated anger came out of me as I punched wildly at my dad. We both ended up covered in gasoline, rolling around on the floor in an awful, embarrassing scuffle.

Big Mama managed to call the fire department. I was taken to the hospital, where they had to use some special fluid to clean out my eyes and ears. I was released that same night; I was too scared to go home so I went to my friend's house to shower and sleep.

When I went home the next day, my dad was sitting in the living room reading the paper and smoking a cigarette. He had cuts all over his face and a black eye.

"Look what you did to me," he said accusingly, looking me straight in the eye.

Like I'm supposed to feel bad? I thought.

"But don't you remember the gasoline?" I said. "Don't you remember threatening to light the house on fire?"

He didn't say anything. I could tell he didn't remember any of those details, as usual. He always seemed to forget the worst things he had done.

I have a lot of stories like that. But my point is not to show that my dad was a terrible person. He wasn't. He was a wounded person and he made terrible mistakes, like many wounded people who are struggling. I have come to terms with my past now. I can think about it without feeling anger or blame. I understand that it's all a part of what made me who I am today, and I wouldn't change that for anything.

That *was* my reality. It feels like I lived with fear more often than not. As a teenager, I didn't need to be 'scared straight.' I was already plenty scared, and committing crime was the last thing on my mind.

My First 'Safety Valve'

Baseball was my escape. All I wanted to do was get a baseball scholarship and become a professional ball player. That was the plan. My dream took a few detours along the way, but I did get a baseball scholarship and later played professionally in Canada. When baseball ended for me, I had to go through a process of finding something that gave me as much passion and drive as baseball had. That journey led me to discover my interest and talent for speaking.

Only recently, I began to see how fear has played such a profound role in my life. On every step of my journey, whether I was on track to my goals or on a detour, I felt fear breathing down the back of my neck. Whether it was the fear of failing or the fear of not being good enough to achieve my dreams, or fear of something terrible I couldn't even name, fear was a space where I lived on a regular basis.

In fact, when I first got to college, I changed my major out of fear. I had been set on becoming a physical therapist, but my first anatomy class intimidated me. I didn't have enough confidence in myself academically. After just one class, one lecture on the first day of school at the University of Utah I decided there was no way I could memorize all the parts of the body we'd have to remember. It was overwhelming; it scared me. I instantly switched my major to sociology and criminal justice, even though I didn't have the same passion for those subjects.

There was the time I got invited to try out for a minor league baseball team and got turned away without getting a chance to prove myself. I was told my name wasn't on the list. To this day, I'm still not sure what error occurred. But instead of *insisting* on my chance to try out, I quietly caved to the pressure, packed my things and got on a plane back home. I could have said, "You haven't picked your team if I'm not on it." Instead, I left without even giving myself a chance to step into the batter's box.

In both of those cases, I let the fear and self-doubt stop me from pursuing my dreams. I didn't know then what I know now. Sometimes you're going to have doubt, and more often than not, you're going to feel fear. That doesn't have to stop you from moving forward; fear and progress *can* co-exist.

CHAPTER THREE: WHAT IS GREATNESS?

I keep using this word Greatness. What do I mean by it? We tend to think of Greatness as meaning being out of the ordinary, extraordinary. You might think of 'the greats' as just a few special people, people like Michael Jordan, Venus and Serena Williams, Muhammad Ali, the WNBA's Kandace Parker, Michael Phelps, Beyoncé, Drake, Bryce Harper and Tom Brady.

But we all have access to Greatness, and that's the type of Greatness I'm talking about in this book. I'm going to show you how to access your Greatness, and how to live from your Greatness every single day.

So what does Greatness look like? Let me start with a story about my son, who I call 'Famous Kobe J.'

Kobe is seventeen, and he's been struggling with health challenges his entire life. Everyone in our life has heard me tell his story, or they've heard it from my wife, Jessica, or our daughter Kendra Jae. Until recently, Kobe hadn't had the chance to really tell his *own* story. When he was fifteen, he saw an opportunity to share his story in front of an audience...and he took it.

My organization, REACH One Alliance, was planning our annual *REACH for Greatness Show*. This is a community event that we put on to raise money for It Takes Guts, a non-profit organization serving families living with pediatric chronic illnesses like Kobe's. We had several amazing performers and speakers on the program including my mentor, the world-renowned motivational icon Les Brown.

Months before the show, I said to Kobe, "I think this is your time to tell your story. Let's put you on the program."

Kobe is not an experienced public speaker yet, but he was up for the challenge. He knew he'd be going in front of an audience of around 900 people, which is a scary thought for just about anyone. Kobe *braced himself.* He began channeling his fear into preparation.

Months in advance, Kobe started writing his speech. He wrote down what he wanted to say, and then he worked on perfecting it. He edited and re-wrote his speech until he had the words just right. Next, he started practicing his speech in front of a mirror, just like I do. He presented his speech to us as a family for feedback and suggestions. He put tens of hours into preparing for the event, reading his speech out loud over and over, practicing and improving his delivery.

One day not long before the show, Kobe and I watched a YouTube video about a local organization called Tower of Niceness. It had been made by two brothers named River and Ryder Sharp in our community, both younger than Kobe. We were impressed with how well the boys spoke, and how authentic they were. Moreover, they were speaking directly to the camera, without any notes. They weren't reading from a page or teleprompter. They were speaking from their hearts, and it was powerful. Their video gave me an idea.

I challenged Kobe to present his talk at the *REACH for Greatness Show* in the same way. I said, "Why don't you go without your notes and speak from your heart? You've been practicing and preparing so much, I know you could do it."

Of course, this was terrifying to him. He had always been planning to bring his speech onstage with him and read what he had prepared. He'd never done anything like this before, and nobody would have judged him one bit for reading his speech. After all, he was a fifteen-year-old kid with no public speaking experience. I told Kobe the final decision was up to him. Right up until the moment he stepped onstage, I didn't know what his choice would be.

When the moment came, 'Famous Kobe J' stepped out onto that stage with his hands empty. No paper. No notes. And he gave an amazing speech, right from the heart. He spoke for seven minutes and he *killed* it. He was humorous, he was authentic, his timing was perfect, and his message was clear. I couldn't have given him one single suggestion for improvement. It was perfect, and he brought the house down. He was absolutely the best version of himself when he got onto that stage and spoke.

Was he scared? You bet. Did he want those notes in front of him? You *know* he did. But did he show up and deliver, from the heart, the best version of himself? Absolutely.

That is what I mean by *Greatness*.

Kobe demonstrated every aspect of Greatness that night. Not just when he stepped out onstage and delivered a great speech, but from the very beginning of the process.

Greatness Is

Best Preparation
Greatness happens in the preparation. It's not just about the moment of achievement. It's all the preparation that leads up to that moment.

When Kobe began writing down his story, he was putting in his Best Preparation. He rehearsed it over and over. He did everything he could to be as prepared as possible. He put in the time. He looked for advice and feedback. He practiced. He committed himself to the preparation. This is one of the most useful ways to channel that fear in your belly. Taking time to prepare is an opportunity for Greatness to show up, even if nobody is watching.

Best Effort

Your Best Effort is just that — *your B*est Effort. It can't be measured by anybody else, but you know what it is for you.

Kobe knew he was putting in his Best Effort in preparing for the speech. He put in his absolute Best Effort on the day of the speech, too. That's part of the reason he was able to demonstrate his Greatness in front of an audience, even though he was scared. The satisfaction of knowing you put your Best Effort into something is its own reward. It doesn't matter if you get the award or the promotion at work or whatever it may be. When you give your Best Effort, you're coming from your Greatness.

Best Focus

Greatness comes when you give your Best Focus in each moment. This means showing up where you need to be and paying attention. It means listening to others in the moment. It means giving your full attention to what you're doing.

If I'm spending time with my family, I need to be focused on that. In order to be the best husband and father I can be, I need to show up with my whole self and Best Focus when I'm with my family. If I'm working on a presentation, I need to bring my Best Focus to the preparation *and* the delivery.

When Kobe J decided to take the leap and deliver his speech without notes, he had to bring his Best Focus into that moment. He was prepared. He was putting in his own Best Effort. He showed up in the moment with *all of himself,* his Best Focus. That's what made it possible for him to throw out the notes. By giving his Best Focus in the moment, he allowed his Greatness to come through.

Best Version of You
More than anything, Greatness is the Best Version of *you*. This is about coming from *your* best place in what you do, moment to moment. It's not about achieving something huge. It isn't about measuring up to someone else's standards. The Best Version of You is operating at your best in small, daily ways. The Best Version of You is the one that will show up and face a challenge even though you're scared. The Best Version of You is the one that listens to that little voice in your head telling you when something is the 'right thing to do,' even if it's not easy.

Let me give you another example. One day, after a long morning at the gym and rushing around to appointments, I had that kind of hunger where you need to eat *right now*! I didn't have a lot of time, so I stopped by a Subway to grab a sandwich. I unwrapped my sandwich as I was exiting the parking lot; I could feel my mouth watering as I was getting ready to take the first bite. I looked left for traffic while simultaneously turning the steering wheel to make a right and, out of the corner of my eye, I saw a homeless person with a sign and a dog. Both the man and the dog looked defeated by life's circumstances. My reaction to what I saw was to hit my brakes and check my rear-view mirror to avoid backing into someone. The Best Version of Me knew the right thing to do in that moment. I rolled down my window and handed the man my meal. Hungry as I was, I knew I had the option to go back and get another one. This guy didn't have that option.

There are moments in life when you just know what the right thing to do is and if you're being the Best Version of Yourself, you'll follow that instinct and do it. It doesn't have to be a public show or win you an award. In fact, it may be something nobody else ever sees you do.

Better Your Best
Better your Best is a mindset. It means you wake up every day deciding that you will do better today than you did yesterday. Every day, you can strive to Better your Best.

At the same time, know that you won't necessarily make huge leaps and bounds in every area every single day. Some days you may fall short, and that's ok. The important thing is to know that, no matter what happened today, you have another opportunity tomorrow. Every day is another chance to Better Your Best.

When Kobe decided to leave his notes behind, he was coming from a Better Your Best mindset. He knew that, as much as he had *already* accomplished, he could do even better. He believed in himself enough to take on the additional challenge. That's the Better Your Best mindset.

Best Skill Set
You may not know yet what your Best Skill Set is, but you have one. It's the thing you do that makes you feel Great just by doing it. It's the area of life where you know you shine. When you're operating in your Best Skill Set, you have that juiced feeling, the feeling that you are right where you should be.

That doesn't mean that it's *easy.* Within your Best Skill Set, you'll have challenges. You'll need to put in the work. You need to show up each day and Better Your Best no matter what.

Now, I don't know what Kobe J's Best Skill Set will turn out to be, but I know he's on the right track to finding it. It took me many years and several different careers to find mine. And even when I *did* decide that speaking was my Best Skill Set, I wasn't good at it right away. I had to apply all kinds of focus,

31

preparation and effort to develop my skills and make a living from them.

In a later chapter, I'll tell the story of finding my Best Skill Set. I'll also share some insights on how to discover *your* Best Skill Set.

Throughout this book, I'll take you through the action steps for getting Scared Great. These are tools I've developed over many years, and I apply in my own life every day. None of these came out of thin air. I'm not going to tell you anything I can't vouch for one hundred percent.

Is Greatness some special thing that only a few people in this world ever get to achieve? Absolutely not. No matter who you are or where you are in life, you have an opportunity each and every single day to show up and BE GREAT.

CHAPTER FOUR: *"FLOAT LIKE A BUTTERFLY, STING LIKE A BEE"*

When I was growing up, I had a constant tape of negativity running through my head. I was always telling myself, "You're not good enough. You're not smart enough, not handsome enough, not talented enough." A lot of the time that negative tape was repeating word for word the things my dad said to me in one of his drunken stupors.

My dad was a passionate man. He loved us *hard*. The love he had for us was palpable, but it wasn't always positive. He was critical. He said negative things. The impact on my self-image was huge.

My mom loved us with passion, but it was a gentle passion. She has always been a soft-spoken, God fearing woman. After she left our dad (and us - my brother and me) and filed for divorce, there wasn't much gentleness left in our house.

That was one of the scariest moments of my young life – coming home and finding all of Mom's clothes gone. After that, we lived with our dad. The environment got a whole lot rougher at that point.

When he was under the influence, my dad often spoke abusive and derogatory words to us. I remember one drive down Watt Avenue with my dad on a drunken rant. He was yelling at me: "You ain't my son – look at you – you's a ugly ass mutha' fucka – look at yo big lips! You look like yo momma – you ain't a Bracy, you're a Tarleton (my Mom's maiden name). Derrick is my son."

I can't recall the reasons for the rants, but I remember hearing those words like it was yesterday. I remember how ugly and unacceptable I already felt as an 11-year-old kid, and those words just made it worse. They stayed with me, continuing to affect my self-esteem as I grew into a teenager.

I still have issues related to the abusive language I heard. I have body image issues to this day due to some of the words spoken to and about me. Today, I'm in the best physical shape of my life, clearly in the upper echelon of fit people, but that's not always what I feel or what I see when I look in the mirror.

What we hear has the power to affect how we see ourselves. I know this first hand. However, I have good news for those who have been affected by experiences similar to mine.

You can reprogram your thinking about yourself. I'm not saying you will forget about what was spoken to you, but you can improve the vision that you have of yourself. You can choose *who* you allow to speak into your life, what events, podcasts and audio programs you choose to take into your mind. And, *you can change what you are saying to yourself* in your own mind. That's where we are going to start in this chapter.

I can't tell you why my dad was compelled to say those kinds of things to my brother and me. Maybe he was trying to make us tough. Maybe he was speaking out loud to us the negativity he was hearing in his own head. I don't know for sure, but it doesn't matter.

It doesn't matter why my dad said those things. Yes, they affected me for a long time. But does that mean I have to be affected by those negative thoughts forever? Does that mean I have to carry around that negative voice and play it constantly in my own head for the rest of my life? No! This is *my* head. These are *my* thoughts. I have the power to change what I think and believe. I have the power to steer my past into a positive direction. I have the power to do this every minute of every day, right now and going forward. That's one of the best things about the way our brains work.

It became a habit to think negative, self-critical thoughts about myself. I had to work to change that habit; I had to work to change those thoughts. Doing that work is what I call *Bracing Myself*, preparing myself to overcome negative thoughts and replace them with positive ones that allow me to be productive and effective in my life.

One of the goals of this book is to show you how to *Brace Yourself* (prepare yourself) with specific *Tools for Greatness*. From here on out, in each chapter of this book, I'm going to show you strategies to accomplish this.

Step one, to begin, we need to *get our minds right*. How? By getting into what I call the Greatness State of Mind.

The Greatness State of Mind

When I was in my teens, my friends and I would sit around and make fun of each other's flaws. We used to call it "capping" when our friends would rip on us. Today's kids might call it "roasting." When you're just joking around with your buddies, it can be funny. But capping on *yourself,* inside your head all the time, isn't going to get you anywhere. It only holds you back.

Self-criticism, self-doubt, and negativity can easily become your way of thinking all the time. It doesn't matter if the negative thoughts are actually true; the more you repeat them to yourself, the more you make them your truth. Anything and everything you continually give mental energy to will become your truth.

Do you see the power in that? That power goes both ways. It means you can *change* where your mental energy is going. You can put forth the effort to mind your thoughts; you can give your mental energy to whatever it is that you *want* to become your truth. You can change the tape that's playing in your head. How do you do this? By taking charge of what you think and say.

When Your Mind Goes Negative, Your Mouth Goes Positive

The late, great Muhammad Ali has always been one of my biggest heroes. What did he think and say? He said, "I am the Greatest." When asked how he boxed, he said, "I float like a butterfly and sting like a bee."

I challenge you to find an example of Muhammad Ali capping on himself! If he had a negative tape running in his mind, he never let any of those statements come out of his mouth. He said, "I am the Greatest." He said, "I'm pretty." He said, "I'm a bad man."

What was Ali doing? He was talking himself into Greatness repeatedly and all the time. The Muhammad Ali mentality is what I call the *Greatness State of Mind*.

It works like this:

- Do not give mental recognition to the possibility of failure, doubt, or defeat.
- When your mind goes negative, your mouth goes positive.
- When your mind says, "I can't," your mouth says "I CAN."
- When your mind says, "I'm not good enough," your mouth says, "I AM good enough."
- When your mind says, "I'm stupid," your mouth says, "I'm brilliant."
- When your mind says, "I just don't feel like I matter," your mouth says, "I DO matter."

Just like Muhammad Ali, you have the power to talk yourself into Greatness. You have *all* the power.

Remember, *when your mind goes negative, your mouth goes positive*. Start noticing that. Bring your mental awareness to noticing when it's happening. When you hear yourself thinking, "I can't do this," catch yourself. Instantly, change that thought to "I CAN do this."

And now I'm going to give away *the* most important secret about the Greatness State of Mind:

It doesn't matter if you *believe* it.
It doesn't *matter* if you believe it.
It doesn't matter if you believe it *yet*.

Just start with changing the words. Every time. Catch yourself. Change the words you are using over and over about yourself, and the belief will change eventually.

What we *think* we are, we *are,* or we're on our way to becoming. The beautiful thing about this is that it is *up to us*. We get to decide how we think of ourselves, how we see ourselves.

Negative thinking is a habit. Positive thinking is a habit. Which habit do you choose to develop? That part is entirely up to you.

Brace Yourself: Tools for Greatness

Throughout this book, I will be presenting you with what I believe are key ways to reach one's Greatness. I've called these "Tools for Greatness," beginning with Tool #1 below.

Brace Yourself
Tools for Greatness
   Tool #1: Create Your Greatness
   Incantations

   Muhammad Ali said, "I am the Greatest."

   Personally, here are some of the things I say to myself:

I'm AWESOME
I'm BRILLIANT
I care ABOUT ME
I'm proud OF ME
I MATTER

In addition, I say this piece I adapted from Og Mandino, *"I will win this day as if it was my last and if it is my last it will be my Greatest moment. This day, today, will be the best day of my life. I will drink each minute until it is full, I will savor the taste and give thanks. I will make each hour count and each minute I will trade only for something of value. I will labor harder than ever before, pushing my mind and my muscles until they cry for relief, and then I will continue. I will love more than ever before, I will live more than ever before. I will serve more than ever before. I will give more than ever before."*

"Procrastination I will destroy with activity. Doubt I will bury

40

though faith and fear I will dismember through action. Each minute of this day will be more fruitful then the hours of yesterday. Our last must be our best. I will win this day as if it was my last, and if it is not, I shall fall to my knees and give thanks."

This **Tool** works for me. Now let's look at you. What are the things you tend to cap on yourself for? As a first step, I suggest you change those negative statements and write a positive version.

Write out the answers to these questions and the next time your mind goes negative, use your answers to make your mind go positive.

- What do you love the most about you?
- What are your best talents?
- What do you do better than anyone else you know?
- What is something you used to consider a flaw about yourself, but you now see as an asset?
- Why do you matter?

Create several Greatness Incantations you can memorize and think about during the day whenever you need them.

CHAPTER FIVE: THE GATEWAYS THAT LEAD TO GREAT WAYS

In the last chapter I talked about how important it is to take charge of what you think and say. Your thoughts and the words you speak are outputs. To take charge of what comes *out of* your mouth, you must take charge of what's going *into* your mind.

We are taking things in and putting things out into the world all the time through what I call the Gateways: Eyes, Ears, Mouth.

We can deliberately direct that process. We can control what we hear, what we read and what we watch. We can also change what comes *out* of our mouths, both towards other people and when we are talking to ourselves. We can choose what influences and energies to let into our hearts and what kind of energy to put back out into the world from our hearts.

That doesn't mean we never feel afraid or have a feeling of low self-esteem or frustration. All of those feelings are human. I'm not trying to teach you how to be some kind of perfect superhuman who never feels fear, self-doubt, disappointment or frustration. That's not even a thing. It doesn't exist.

We are all human, and we are going to feel fear, doubt, disappointment and frustration. What we *can* control is what we do with those feelings. What we *can* do is channel those feelings into making ourselves the best versions of ourselves each day. We *can* use those feelings to steer ourselves into Greatness.

How? First, we can consciously take charge of the GATEWAYS, starting with the eyes.

Eye Gate: Leaders are Readers, Writers are Mentors

When you read the testimonials on the back of any book, you'll notice that those quotes come from leaders of the world. You'll also notice that most who write books are leaders as well. If you have aspirations of ever becoming a leader – congratulations! The fact that you're reading *SCARED GREAT* means you are one or are on your way to becoming one.

How would you like to have your pick of mentors from a huge pool of incredibly talented, motivated, wise, knowledgeable and experienced leaders in their fields? And what if those mentors didn't even need you to call them up or make an appointment; what if you could meet with them on your own time?

You can! Reading their books makes them accessible to you whenever you want them to be. Remember, you have to read to lead!

Many teachers, motivators, authors, parents and coaches talk about the importance of mentors. Many people who aspire to be professional speakers have reached out to me asking for mentorship over the years. I have benefited more than I can say from those who have mentored me.

A GREAT mentor is not easy to find. But I don't believe you 'find' mentors exactly. I believe you attract the mentors you seek by pursuing what you really want to do, by committing to your dreams and by putting in the work to study and prepare.

And I have some great news for you – until you attract the mentor you're seeking, you have access to a deluge of mentors who will show up for you 24 hours a day, 7 days a week, 365 days a year.

To find this vast network of mentors, you have only to be willing to read. It's necessary to find the time to slow down, to resist the many distractions of Facebook, Instagram, Twitter, Snapchat and so on. Pick up a book – whether you read it on your Kindle, read a hard copy or download an audio book, your willingness to turn to books will make an endless array of potential mentors instantly available to you.

Moreover, reading benefits you in a host of additional ways:

- Reading stimulates the mind and inspires the heart.
- Reading is the water that washes away the flame of fear when it rises inside you.
- Reading connects you with ideas and possibilities bigger than you can imagine on your own.
- Reading positions you to find the words that inspire you and bring you hope, words that enhance your vision, help you reach your goals and keep you feeling motivated.

When I first read Dexter Yager's book, *Don't let Anyone Steal Your Dream,* it shifted my entire psyche and imagination about the possibilities for my life. In that book, Yager pointed out a simple but powerful thought – every building you see, every piece of clothing you wear, every car you drive, every object around you has been created by humans. All of these things are the products of someone's imagination.

Something clicked in my mind that caused me, at that moment, to dream beyond sports. Ever since that day, I've been a dreamer. I became more aware of creative power, a power we *all* have. This creative power allows me to envision anything, everything. I know that once I'm able to picture something I want in my mind, I can work towards that vision and ultimately bring it about with consistent faith and effort.

Without Dexter Yager mentoring me through his book, I would not have had that realization. I didn't need to sit down with him to get face-to-face mentorship from him to gain this invaluable perspective. All I had to do was read his book.

I'd like to take a moment here to thank some of my mentors who, through their books, have shown up to coach me on my schedule: I am grateful to:

- ✧ Dr. Norman Vincent Peale, *The Power of Positive Thinking*
- ✧ The Late Great Stephen Covey, *Greatness Everyday*
- ✧ David J. Swartz, *The Magic of Thinking Big*
- ✧ Dexter Yager, *Don't Let Anybody Steal Your Dream*
- ✧ Russell Simmons, *Do You! 12 Laws to Access the Power in You to Achieve Happiness and Success*
- ✧ Willie Jolley, *A Setback Is A Set Up for A Comeback*
- ✧ Les Brown, *It's not Over Until You Win* and *Live Your Dreams*
- ✧ Harvey McKay, *Swim with the Sharks Without Being Eaten Alive*
- ✧ Anthony Robbins, *Awaken the Giant Within*

- John C. Maxwell, *17 Irrefutable Laws of Leadership*
- Jack Canfield, *Success Principles*
- Dottie Walters, *Speak and Grow Rich*
- Michael Jeffreys, *Success Secrets of the Motivational Super Stars,*
and many, many others.

These authors became my mentors before I had the privilege of meeting any of them in person. They filled my mind and heart with hope, promise, inspiration and empowerment while I was in pursuit of my dream. They gave me insight, knowledge and practical strategies for working on myself *and* becoming skilled in my profession, which are really one and the same thing. These author-mentors helped me develop in the way I needed in order to attract mentors in person. I encourage you to check them out – they might just change your life too.

Ear Gate: Reprogram Your Thinking with Audio

The words I grew up hearing had a profound impact on my self-image. It took many years into adulthood before I realized I had the power to change that self-image by changing the words I was hearing, both internally and externally.

My first in-person mentor appeared at a time in my life when I was still full of negative thinking. I was fearful, lacking in self-confidence, still hearing that old tape of negativity, criticism, and self-doubt that had been stuck in my head since childhood. When I began to work with Ken Westenskow (aka, The Big Legend) that tape finally started to change.

It was before my second season playing professional baseball. I had been worrying about life after baseball – what was I going to do next? I had a family to support and needed to be forward thinking. Through a chance series of events, I got involved with multi-level marketing and had been working on that new skill set whenever I wasn't playing ball. That was how I met Ken; he generously coached me on how to become a better entrepreneur and think like a winner. Part of that process was helping me to build my confidence and self-esteem, which are so crucial for anyone who wants to be successful in business.

Ken introduced me to a personal development regimen. His prescription consisted of the following:

1. Listen to one motivational audio program per day.
2. Read for at least fifteen minutes per day.
3. Attend one live business and/or personal development seminar per month.
4. Have a sit down conversation with him once a month.

As an aside, Ken told me, "If you listen to these audio programs during the off season, your batting average is going to skyrocket along with your confidence when you're in season." And he was absolutely right – It did!

Notice that Ken's regimen had nothing to do with fitness or physical training. It was all about mental training and reprogramming negative beliefs.

That year I played the best baseball of my entire career. As a result of a growing belief in myself, my game went to a new level. I had increased confidence simply due to the positive messages I was choosing to expose myself to over and over.

I had always worked hard on the baseball field. That was not the thing that changed. What made the difference was that I was starting to re-shape the way I thought about myself and about my abilities. What changed was that I actually started to FEEL hopeful and positive, instead of anxious and afraid and hard on myself.

I also worked my butt off in the weight room during the off-season, so when the season started, I was ready to roll. My first at-bat in spring training was against our number one pitcher, Darren Spiller. He was a soft-throwing, crafty lefty who knew how to hit spots. He had a sneaky fastball that could bust you inside and break your bat.

Darren knew that my weakness was getting my hands through the zone on an inside fastball, so of course that's what he threw me - an inside fastball. For the first time, I had the confidence to spin on that sucker and I hit it out of the yard with power I didn't know I had!

At that moment, Ken's words about my increased confidence were confirmed. That was how my spring training started, and I took that momentum throughout the year.

I continued listening to audio programs with inspiring messages in order to change the negative voices in my head. I was reconditioning my whole way of thinking in a fundamental and profound way, by bombarding myself with positive messages.

I literally and intentionally started listening to four or five positive messages per day. I did that for about five years on a consistent basis. That habit influenced the entire trajectory of my life and has affected the next generation of my family too because it has helped define my life and how I raise my children.

You would be stunned to hear the positivity that comes from my children. It is completely different from the thoughts I had and the words that used to come out of my own mouth when I was a scared kid. Both my daughter Kendra and my son Kobe J are among the most positive people you could ever meet. They are amazing. In part, I attribute their optimism and kindness to the fact that I, their dad, did some work to reprogram my own negative thought patterns in ways that helped me not pass on my former negative thinking to them.

I can't overstate the importance of audio programs on my journey from *Scared* to *Scared Great*. In fact, those audios were what planted the dream of becoming a motivational speaker into my heart. If I had to give you a top five list of what has influenced my life for the better, listening to audio programs would be either number one or number two on that list.

I've heard it said that the average person thinks approximately 50,000 to 80,000 thoughts per day and 80% of those thoughts are negative. One of the habits necessary to change that staggering number of negative thoughts is to invest the time in developing yourself via listening to podcasts daily.

The right words guard us against the negative 'chatter' coming from all around us, whether it's coming from co-workers, people we encounter every day, the news, the Internet, our parents, our friends, or from advertising. So much of these audio inputs are conveying a message of fear, anxiety, self-criticism, dissatisfaction, and pessimism – all forms of negativity. It is crucial to balance out all that chatter with *positivity*.

Just as we learn to build ourselves up with the way we speak to ourselves, it's imperative to make sure that a lot of what we take in through our ear gates is *building us up* too.

Listen…Re-Listen…Listen….Re-Listen…to words that empower you with hope, a better attitude and a productive mindset. Being open and coachable to taking in these types of words will steer you towards your personal Greatness. It did for me and I'm 100% sure it's doable for you too.

Mouth Gate: When Mind Goes Negative, Mouth Goes Positive

In the next chapter, we will focus more on the Mouth Gate. For now, as you seek to build your own Greatness Mindset on a daily basis, remember that what you say, to yourself and others, needs to be positive and supportive of your best self. Continue to hold the crucial thought that, *when your mind goes negative, your mouth goes positive.*

To start taking charge of your Gateways, I suggest you *Begin Your Day the Greatness Way* and *End Your Night with Momentum in Sight,* described below. Each one takes just twenty minutes; together they can be easily used to bookend each day. They will have a positive effect, no question about it, on everything that happens in between.

Early on in my journey to becoming a professional speaker I'd take short trips to Palm Springs on my own. I spent the time studying, writing, thinking, praying, concentrating, working, listening, focusing, willing and speaking my dreams into reality. I did this because I thought it was important to stop and invest 'laser beam' focused time on my dreams and goals amid the busyness of life.

With help from some of the world's top spiritual leaders and personal development gurus whose words and wisdom I was ingesting into my Gateways, I gradually developed a specific process for starting my day. Anthony Robbins, Joel Osteen and Wayne Dyer are the speakers who had the most impact on my developing this process. Anthony Robbins talks about the importance of how you begin your day. He calls it the "Hour of Power." Joel Osteen writes about the importance of being grateful and having a communication with God in the morning. I began to incorporate those principles into my morning routine.

In Palm Springs, I started a habit of getting up early and going for a slow, methodical walk to *Brace Myself,* meaning, *prepare* myself for the day. The idea was to guide my energy in a focused direction before the hustle and bustle of the day took over.

That was over twelve years ago. I've evolved and streamlined the process over the last twelve years into a simple formula that I call *Begin Your Day the Greatness Way*, also known as *20 Minutes Alone to Plug into Your Greatness Zone.*

Brace Yourself
Tools *for Greatness*
   Tool #2: Begin your Day the
   Greatness Way
   Or, 20 Minutes Alone to Step into
   Your Greatness Zone

   To *Begin Your Day the Greatness Way*, get up, get out and go for a 20-minute walk. Do whatever you need to do the night before to make sure you can get out of bed and get started, whether it's setting the alarm a little earlier, laying out your clothes, or putting your shoes by the door if that's what it takes to get you going. Set yourself up so that it will be easy to *Begin Your Day the Greatness Way*.

   On this 20-minute walk, you're going to dedicate 5 minutes to each of the following:

      5 minutes of *Silence*

5 minutes of *Gratitude*
5 minutes of *Greatness Incantations*
5 minutes of *Visualization*

Silence: Research shows that it is beneficial to spend at least 15 minutes of conscious silence in every 24 hours. This is a time to be alert and aware, but also relaxed and not striving for anything. This isn't time to be thinking or doing; it's time to push all negativity, doubt and anxiety out of your mind. It's just that – *silence*.

As Wayne Dyer says, "The wind whispers secrets to us in the mornings but we have to be awake and outside in order to hear them."

Gratitude: Who and what are you grateful for? Speak it out loud.

There is a wealth of scientific research showing that gratitude equals a greater sense of wellbeing and happiness. Grateful people are healthier, and they are more likely to achieve their goals. They are also more likely to enjoy their lives on a daily basis.

For the second five minutes of your walk, name all the things you're grateful for. Focus on that feeling. You might consider saying to yourself:

"I'm grateful for my family, I'm grateful for the fact that there is food in the refrigerator, that I have access to running water, that I'm able to work towards my dreams, that I live in the U.S.A., that I can become whatever I'm willing to work for, that I have shoes on my feet, that I have a shirt on my back, that I woke up this morning, that I have the ability to walk, that I have the ability to talk, grateful to be alive and upright"... and so on.

Affirm Your Greatness: Encourage yourself. Talk yourself *up*. Get yourself into the Greatness State of Mind.

While I'm on my walk, I say things like:

"Kevin, you are the best at what you do. You are living your dream. You are ready to better your best today. You are going to win the day. You can overcome whatever life challenges you will face today. You change lives when you speak. You are going to encourage everyone within your wing span today. You will make a difference in someone's life today."

We have to create a positive feedback loop for ourselves by *actively and proactively* changing any habitual negative thoughts. It's not a passive process. Use your Greatness from the last chapter, or any positive statements you think of in the moment. Remember, you don't even have to *believe* it *yet*.

Visualization: Visualize a mellifluous flow to your day. *'Mellifluous'* means to be like a perfect melody - flowing like honey – harmonious, smooth, rich, tuneful.

Take five minutes to visualize your entire day flowing mellifluously. Visualize having a positive impact on every person you talk to. Visualize everything you do going well. Picture yourself being effective in all your encounters.

Visualize that which you *want* to *BE*. Give no mental energy to the possibility of failure, doubt or defeat. It doesn't matter if your day actually goes that way – it may not – it probably won't. That's not the point. The point is to focus on where you are putting your mental energy.

Visualization is powerful. It's my experience that the things I've visualized and spoken out during my *20 Minutes Alone* have become realities in my life today. I'm not saying that to brag. I'm saying it because it is a simple fact about the power of visualization.

Les Brown said, "Thoughts have magnetic power; what you focus on the longest becomes the strongest." Focus on making each day a Great day!

CHAPTER SIX: CARRY IT IN YOUR HEART – SPEAK IT WITH YOUR MOUTH

In the last chapter I talked about what you're taking *IN*. My question to you now is: What are you putting *OUT*?

> **Heart:** Bombarding yourself with positivity changes what's in your heart.

> **Mouth:** Expressing gratitude, talking yourself up, speaking your dreams and visions, *instead* of your fears, changes what's in your heart.

What's in your heart? What's coming out of your mouth? Do you believe in yourself yet? You *can* develop that belief in your heart and speak it with your mouth. How do you do that? By taking charge of your Eye and Ear Gateways you will change for the better what you believe in your heart and that will affect your Mouth Gateway, what comes out of your mouth.

I have had some of the most powerful moments of my life while taking in the stories of others, including leaders, speakers, writers, entertainers, teachers and children. Choosing to listen to, watch, read, and speak to others who have hope and who have made their dreams come true can fill your own heart with positivity and hope.

As I've noted before and need to keep stressing here, what you carry in your heart will manifest in your words and actions. As you internalize hopefulness, you will become someone who has a positive impact on the people around you. This will steer you to your Greatness.

The flipside is obvious. If you are surrounded by negativity, if you choose to read, watch and listen only or mainly to things on TV and/or social media that radiate negativity and hopelessness, that is what you will carry in your heart. *You have the choice!* You get to choose what you are going to expose yourself to, what you want to be around. You can choose hopefulness and avoid negativity.

Bombard Your Eye and Ear Gates at the Same Time: Attend Seminars

I love attending talks and seminars. Through them, I have been exposed to an endless array of ideas, strategies, stories and insights that have led directly to positive changes in my life. I'm an emotional guy; watching and hearing people tell their stories in real life is paramount for me. It helps me internalize the belief that I can make positive changes for myself.

I remember moments at seminars when I've been so filled with the emotion of hope that I was crying, feeling I had just 'cracked the code' to my own

Greatness, believing anything was possible and success was imminent if I just didn't give up.

In fact, those experiences led me to my own personal definition of the *American Dream*. For me, the *American Dream* is the mere recognition that there are more opportunities than I, by myself, could possibly take advantage of at any given moment for the rest of my life. Another way to say this is to put into three words…. *ANYTHING IS POSSIBLE*.

The Power of Positive Words

I'll never forget being in the Anaheim Duck Pond Arena at a seminar, listening to a speaker named Brad De Haven tell his story. He was describing his and his wife's journey to success and financial freedom. Brad talked about creating a personal incantation and he shared his with us.

That day, I realized that the power of affirming language was even greater than I knew. As I explained before, in your personal incantation you speak what you want as if it *has already happened*. An incantation isn't a promise to do something, a belief that you will do something one day. It isn't a goal or a dream. It is a factual statement describing your heart's deepest desire in words as the truth, in the present tense. The very act of speaking this incantation brings it more and more into your reality, makes it exist. The more you affirm this as your truth, the truer it becomes to *YOU*. That's what matters....*YOU BELIEVE IT*!

This experience was so inspiring to me that I instantly started creating an incantation of my own. My incantation is:

> "Life Changers International has absolutely exploded. I choose to read from a positive book every single day no matter how busy or tired I am. I listen to an audio every day and, through blessings from God, I have become the epitome of a people builder.

> "I make a conscious, deliberate, determined effort to give each individual with whom I come in contact something uplifting and from my heart. I prospect new business with ease; making cold calls is a piece of cake. I attend all business functions with the specific intent to listen, to learn and to implement. I knew it would take work, discipline, love, patience and consistency to make my dreams real.

> "My wife Jessica is truly my queen. I respect her. I love to hug her. I enjoy taking time out of my schedule to look her in the eyes and tell her how much I love her.

"I built this business to leave a legacy of wisdom and wealth to my progeny – wisdom as it relates to my love for God Almighty, my love for people, a non-judgmental attitude, leadership skills, communication skills, 'get-to-it-iveness', 'stick-to-it-iveness,' entrepreneurship, passion, discipline, goal setting and goal getting."

Life Changers International (LCI) was born through the truth that words changed my life. The LCI tagline – *Changing Lives Through the Power of Positive Words* – comes from personal experience, because the words I have consistently attended to over time have had the power to change the trajectory of my entire life.

Once it became a habit for me to speak to myself differently, then it became a reflex for me to work to build up others.

Changing the Tape

Many years ago, my life was changed completely by something that reached me via the Ear Gateway. My first mentor, Ken Westenskow, who I told you about in Chapter Five, had given me an audio to listen to. It was one of the many audio programs Ken passed on to me at the time, when he was working with me to build my confidence in business and, coincidentally, as a baseball player.

But this particular audio, unlike any of the others, happened to get stuck in the tape deck of the white Pontiac I was driving then. I literally could not eject it or pry it out, so the tape played every time I turned on the car. It was Les Brown's "It's Not Over Until You Win."

This tape played all the time, over and over, for four months. I heard it so often I practically memorized it. In fact, it got to the point I was kind of tuning it out; nonetheless, Les's message was still reaching me. Slowly but surely, the message on Les's audio was changing and *replacing* the hopeless, fearful tape of negativity that had been playing silently in my head for years. I found that I was excited to get into my car just because of how the tape made me feel.

Hearing those words repeatedly, day after day, slowly but surely dripped and dripped on my brain and created a profound shift in my consciousness as well as a shift in my attitude about myself. I became a more positive person; my outlook on life became more positive. My mind, which had previously been closed, too often by fear, began to open to new ideas, new vistas. I was open to new possibilities, and that's why, I believe, I had my epiphany moment.

I had been listening to this audio, driving around working on my business, for *months.* But one day, something about it struck me differently. I was hit so hard by my realization that I had to pull over and get off the road. My hands were shaking.

I realized that all Les Brown was doing was *telling his story*. And all I had to do was figure out *how to tell mine*.

I was awakened to a possibility I had never imagined. The messages I had been taking in had changed what was in my heart. Telling my story seemed possible. In fact, it seemed like it just might be the thing I wanted to do more than anything else, maybe even more than playing baseball.

That moment was just the beginning, a *seed* of an idea that would become a life-long journey and my purpose. That seed would never have been planted if I had not heard the words, had not allowed the words that changed the internal dialogue (my inner voice) that was playing in my mind.

Mentors Are All Around You

A lot of us are looking for mentors. I have had several. A lot of the kids I work with need father figures. It's a fact. It may not always be easy to find the mentor you need in real life but, as we have previously discussed, mentors are all around us. So, even if you don't yet have a mentor you personally know, don't let that stop you from being inspired by the leaders you read or hear about, admire and look up to.

As I've told you, Les Brown's voice changed my life long before I ever met him. Eventually I did get to know him personally *and* he became – and continues to be - a mentor to me. That's the kind of thing that happens when you are using your Gateways in the right ways. You will find your mentors and/or they will find you.

Keep on Keeping On

After my second season of playing baseball, I shifted my focus and energy to building a business. As that journey began, I was so impatient. I wanted immediate success, immediate gratification. I wanted to see the money everyone talked about and I wanted it right away. I didn't want to wait.

Being new to entrepreneurship, at first, I didn't understand I'd have to build myself up, build my attitude and build my confidence, all while building the business. Ken was my mentor; he helped me keep my thinking straight; his coaching was invaluable. I have carried his coaching and his messages with me through all my efforts as an entrepreneur and a professional speaker. Ken helped me develop long-term thinking and taught me delayed gratification. I can still hear Ken telling me that it was all about needing to keep on keeping on.

Here's what delayed gratification looks like. With Ken I learned that the entrepreneurial process was work, work, work, work, work, work, work, work, work, work, work, work, work, work, work, work, get paid, work, work, work, work, work, work, work, work, work, work, work, work, work, get paid, work, work, work, work, work, work, work, work, work, get paid, work, get paid, work, get paid, work, get paid...and then eventually you'll work, get paid, get paid, get paid, get paid, get paid, get paid, get paid...all while you work.

Without Ken's coaching and perspective, I never would have gotten to the 'get paid' part. He taught me that an entrepreneurial mindset is antithetical to the employee mindset. An entrepreneurial mindset means you're not just doing a job for which you'll get a pay check; it means you have to have faith that your hard work will pay off, even if you don't see a profit for years. It takes patience and consistent, specific action.

It takes faith that achievement is possible, even if you aren't where you want to be right away. It takes an investment in each moment of your journey, because you know in your heart that it's worth it.

It doesn't matter what your goal is, whether or not it has anything to do with building a business. The same principles apply to anything you want in life, any creative effort, any attempt to be happier or more at peace, any project related to family, faith or fitness, any situation where you feel *fear* of failure, *fear* of loss.

That *fear* is normal, and it is powerful. How can you steer and direct that *fear*? By paying attention and making choices EVERY DAY to the messages that you let into your EYES and EARS, by tending to what you carry in your HEART, and by what you speak into the world with your MOUTH.

"Keep on keeping on," Ken Westenskow taught me. I'm passing it on to you. Keep re-reading that until you internalize it and make it your own.

Brace Yourself:
Tools for Greatness
Tool #3: End your Night with Momentum in Sight

Do you have a process for going to bed at night? What do you do in those last minutes before bed?

The last twenty minutes before going to bed are as important and as useful as the first twenty minutes of the day. Why not use this time in a conscious and deliberate way? It's a perfect opportunity to fill your Gateways with positivity.

Think about structuring the end of your day with:

5 minutes of Reflection: Reflect on your gratitude, even if it's just the gratitude of having lived another day. What did you learn? Reflect on that. What could you have done better? Take this time to reflect *without* harsh self-criticism or judgment. Just notice honestly if there is something you could have done better. Reflect on how you're going to approach tomorrow.

5 minutes of Journaling: Harvey McKay taught me that life gives us three lessons per day, and the only way to truly absorb those lessons is to write them down. He said his bestselling books, particularly *How to Swim with Sharks Without Being Eaten Alive*, are collections of his daily life lessons in book form. I'm not trying to say you have to write a book; I'm just encouraging you to document your life lessons each day. A great way to do that is by taking five minutes to jot them down before you fall asleep.

5 minutes of Prayer/Gratitude: This doesn't have to be religious prayer necessarily, just whatever works for you. This is about giving thanks for all the people, situations, opportunities, progress and productivity your day had within it.

5 minutes of Reading: Lay your eyes on something that is peaceful and soothing to your mind, body and spirit before you rest. Screens are not good for rest, and neither is the news. Blue light is not going to help you have a restful sleep. Take the last five minutes before bed to look at something comforting and inspiring.

What we take into our minds at the end of the day, and what we focus on, is what we will bring into our sleep and into the next day. Make sure it's positive.

When you *Begin Your Day the Greatness Way*, and *End Your Night with Momentum in Sight*, you are living with purpose and intentionality which is maximizing the time you have on this earth to live the life you want to live. Brace Yourself to Win the Days ahead.

CHAPTER SEVEN: WIN THE DAY

Life is about finding joy in the journey. Everybody likes winning. Winning creates a feeling of happiness. You can strive each day to reach a goal, to have each day be a win, no matter what long-term vision or dream you have as your big picture. By doing that you hold yourself accountable to maximize your moments; you operate from the certainty that each 'today' matters. Each day working toward your goal is full of opportunity, the chance to show up with, as we talked about in Chapter 3, your *Best Focus, Best Effort, Best Version of You*. You take advantage of the chance to *Better Your Best* every day.

After my very first Toastmaster's talk, that I'll tell you about in a little while, I knew exactly what I wanted to do with my life. I knew I wanted to be a professional speaker. But as I realized that, I also realized there was a huge chasm between the emotion I felt -- my desire to reach that goal -- and my knowledge of HOW to do it. I had no experience, no connections. I hadn't gone to school for anything close to that. I had just given my first speech ever. I was most assuredly a beginner.

I was determined to start the process and learn whatever I had to do to reach my goal, but it wasn't easy. There were times I felt like I was making no progress, seeing no opportunities. I was blinded by frustration because I wasn't 'there' yet. I was scared I would never get 'there.' I was working hard but I didn't have joy in my heart; I was so worried about getting wherever 'there' was that I wasn't enjoying the journey, even though I was committed to it.

In my family, we used to have a little ritual for New Year's Eve. Every December 31st Jessica, daughter Kendra, Kobe J and I would each write down our personal goals for the year and then put them into sealed envelopes. We'd place the envelopes in a drawer in the kitchen where we'd leave them for the year.

The next New Year's Eve, we'd take the envelopes out and look at what we had written. We'd see whether we had achieved our goals and we'd celebrate when we had. It was fun to write the goals down, to look back later and check on our successes. It was satisfying to celebrate the goals we had achieved.

One year, I went over to the drawer, got my envelope out as usual, and went to sit in my spot on the couch. For the first time, I had an anti-climactic feeling. Even though I had achieved the goals on my list, I didn't find that satisfying. I realized I didn't like waiting a whole year to celebrate my progress. I'm an impatient guy; I discovered I wanted to create a way to keep score of wins and losses every day!

My takeaway? There's no reason to wait a whole year to feel you've accomplished something or to celebrate your achievements. Why not celebrate your progress, even if it's infinitesimal, *every day*?

When you show up every day, opportunities and connections show up too. Often these opportunities are the exact things you might miss if you are thinking only about the future or some future goal. Don't miss out; notice your progress *every day*!

Achieving your Dreams is a Process

When you realize you want something, you may also be aware there's a chasm between goals and abilities, between what you want and what you know how to achieve. That is often the case; in fact, it might be a constant in life. In my case, when I decided I wanted to be a speaker who inspired others with my story, I recognized right away that I did not have the necessary skill set to accomplish that -- yet.

I had the skill set to play baseball and had been doing it professionally for two years. I had the skill set for social work because that's what I studied in school. I had begun developing the skill set required to start a business, thanks to my mentor Ken and my growing experience in entrepreneurship. But I simply did not have the information, the practice, or the skills to be a professional speaker.

Did I let that discourage me? Sometimes, yes! There was a period of time when I felt pretty frustrated. I was so excited by the feeling that speaking gave me, and so eager to get started, and it was frustrating to admit that I wasn't there yet.

As with anything else I had learned, I knew I would have to work to acquire the skills necessary to become a professional speaker. I had to focus on the reality that, no matter how good a person may become at something, or how right it feels to do a certain thing, being exceptional at it does not happen *overnight*. All of the 'greats' in any field you can think of had to put in the time and the work to get there, to become exceptional.

I like to think the key is to make *Consistent Infinitesimal Progress (C.I.P.)* towards your goals. In my definition of C.I.P., "consistent" means *daily*, "infinitesimal" means *very small* and "progress" means *moving forward*. And all forward movement is a plus.

But What Do You Do in the Meantime?

What happens in the chasm between a dream and developing the necessary skills to live that dream? Are you just waiting? Working? Looking forward to one day in the future when the work pays off? Are you hyper-focused on the end goal to the extent that you're not enjoying each day of your life?

I certainly do not recommend that approach. I believe strongly that we have to be happy on the journey. That's all life is; the journey is the whole thing. We can't make it "I'll be happy when I get there."

In the immortal words of Muhammad Ali, "The fight is won or lost far away from witnesses -- behind the lines, in the gym, and out there on the road, long before I dance under those lights."

It's Not Every Four Years -- It's Every Day

The moment I walked onto the campus of the Olympic Training Center in Colorado Springs, I was in awe, for two reasons. First, it was surreal to me that I would soon be speaking on the Center's stage, the same stage as Olympic Gold Medalist Billy Mills. In fact, I was scheduled to speak right after him.

It was 1999, still relatively early in my career as a professional speaker. Every time I was given an opportunity like this was incredible to me. It still is to this day. I'm still in awe of how far I've come on this journey. If I went back in time and told that scared kid huddled in a corner of a couch in a dark duplex in Sacramento, that one day he'd be getting paid to speak on a stage with Olympic Gold Medalists, I don't think that kid would have believed me.

The other reason for my awe was the incredible size and grandness of the campus. For a moment, I felt like I was standing in the middle of Times Square, minus the traffic noise. I slowly spun around, taking in the moment. Enormous banners, reading IT'S NOT EVERY FOUR YEARS. IT'S EVERY DAY, hung on each building in all directions in which I looked.

Those words have stuck with me ever since. They say so much about the power of a single day, so much about the work ethic, the passion, patience, consistency, love and heart of all those athletes who train for the Olympics.

When we watch the Olympic Trials and the Games, what we see are top-notch, mind- blowing athletes performing with their bodies at optimal levels. What we *don't* see is what they put themselves through, day in and day out, to get there. We don't see the everyday training, the work and dedication that goes into preparing for *years* for a competition that, in most cases, lasts only for seconds.

Those words come back and reverberate through my mind from time to time, reminding me that it's not about rushing to get to the goal, dream or vision. It's about who I am today, who I'm becoming. It's about the Greatness I work at every day, not just on game day. It's about the *process*. To have joy on the journey, I need to focus on the *process*, not just the end goal.

The Process is Everything

Eight years after that day at the Olympic Training Center, I learned another incredible lesson from top tier Olympic athletes. In 2007, I signed a development deal to host my own talk show: *The Kevin Bracy Show*. During the brainstorming process to decide the 'who,' 'what' and 'where' of the pilot episode, the executive producer Cort Cassady sent me out on assignments to interview various people.

My first assignment was to interview two athletes, one male and the other female, who were training to compete in Beijing for the August 2008 Olympics. I began to cogitate about what questions to ask them in the interviews. I thought I had two great, 'no-brainer' questions ready to ask each of them:

1. Does the image of you standing on that podium in Beijing, bending over as the official places the Gold Medal around your neck, drive you and consume your thoughts as you train?
2. Do you believe you will be competing in Beijing on 8/8/08?

I asked these questions to both Olympic hopefuls the same day, at different times. In both cases, I was completely surprised by the answers. Both athletes said the same thing; both, in a word, said NO.

In response to the first question, each of them told me they were not consumed by the image of the gold medal. Far from it. Each athlete said, essentially, "The only thing I focus on is perfecting the process. The only thing that controls whether I stand on that podium or not is my performance in that day, in that moment."

One of the Olympic hopefuls said, "Naturally my mind goes there, but I consciously, immediately pull myself back to what's important. I focus on every repetition in the weight room, every meal to fuel my body, every stride between hurdles in practice, every breath between strides. The process is more important than the result. When I perfect the process, I will get the result I want."

As for my next 'no-brainer' question about *belief*, both athletes told me there was no focus on *belief* at all, for either of them. "*Belief* is a non-factor; it has nothing to do with this," one said. "The *process* is everything."

My first thought in that moment was, "Man, I wish I had this type of mindset when I was playing sports!" The next thing I thought was, "How can I apply this mindset to my journey of growing my speaking brand?"

Define Your Focus -- Win the Day

You don't have to focus on winning the race or the contest; you need to focus on *Winning the Day*. What does it mean to win the day? It means showing up with your *Best Version of You*, your *Best Focus* and *Best Effort;* it means *Bettering your Best*, each day, every day.

Life is a process. Reaching your goals is a process. Living your dreams is a process. We have to show up to the process every single day. We steer our fear every single day. We find the value in every day, not just when we've reached some huge achievement. Finding joy on the journey *is* the achievement.

Brace Yourself
Tools for Greatness
Tool #4: Identify and Define Your Daily Focus Areas (DFAs)

We've got to find value in each day. That's what I mean by *Winning the Day*. So how do you set yourself up to Win the Day? You have to identify your Daily Focus Areas (DFAs). You do that by asking yourself, "What are the most important areas of *my* life?"

One day, when legendary speaker Willie Jolley was speaking in my

80

hometown of Sacramento, he very kindly reached out to me to tell me he was in my neck of the woods. I went to visit him at a hotel with all my questions ready to ask him. We were sitting by the pool and I asked, "Willie what action and areas do I need to focus on every day to grow my business?" He said, "We all juggle a lot of things every day. We have many balls in the air at any given time. Ask yourself 'which of those balls are made of glass? Which of them can you NOT afford to drop?'

As we've talked about before, we have approximately 17 hours of functionality in a day. Within those hours, we must determine the Daily Focus Areas (DFAs) that we intend to pay attention to in order to bring out the Best Version of ourselves.

Identify Your Daily Focus Areas (DFAs):

Your first step will be to select, decide on, identify your DFAs. I've identified mine; I have six. I call them my Significant 6. For you, it might be your Super 7 or your Fabulous 5 or your Necessary 9 -- whatever areas you decide are the most important to you.

To give you some examples, I'll take you through mine. Again, keep in mind that yours may be, probably will be, different.

My DFAs are:

1. **Family**: It could be 5 seconds, 5 minutes or 5 hours, but I need to connect with my family. My wife is hilarious -- she should be on stage doing stand-up comedy -- and we like to laugh. I need to spend time with Jessica and have a real, gut-wrenching, stomach muscle cramping laughs with her at least once a day for that connection. I have to check in with my son and do our little back and forth silliness to make my connection with him. My daughter lives in Los Angeles and we make our connection through a daily phone conversation. If I don't authentically connect with my family, then I can't say I'm the best version of me that day nor

can I Win the Day without that connection.

2. **Faith:** I have to connect with my faith, whether through giving thanks, silence, prayer, music, meditation or reading my bible. Every day, I need to connect with the power of God. When I miss this connection, my life sometimes feels empty and dark.

3. **Fitness:** I need to have some connection with my health and fitness. If I miss my workout, I can't say I'm the best version of me that day. I need that ingredient. If I miss it, that's ok, but I can't say I won the day, and I know what I need to do tomorrow.

4. **Finance:** Each day I need to think about building my business, connecting with others, putting work in on some project, and/or preparing for a presentation or an opportunity. Every day I need to ensure I'm in alignment with the legacy that I want to build and leave for my children.

5. **Future**: I need to take a moment to glance into the future. I ask myself, what's coming up and am I on track for that thing? What do I need to do today to prepare for that talk I'm giving next week, next month or that documentary or that book I'm working on? I check in with the future, but I don't spend a lot of time there, just as much as I need to be prepared.

6. **Fundraising**: To be the best version of me, I need to work on or create an opportunity for our family cause, our non-profit, It Takes Guts. This cause is bigger than my business, my brand, my family, my personal sphere. I need to be thinking about how to generate money or resources in a way that helps other people and my community.

I need to check in with those 6 Daily Focus Areas to know whether I Won the Day.

Define Your Daily Focus Areas (DFAs)

After you have identified your DFAs, your next task is to define them, spell them out in detail for yourself. Defining what each of your DFAs is the way to ensure you've got the right ones. Only you can do it. To do it well, make sure you 'go deep.'

To define your DFAs, ask yourself three questions:

1. **What** do I want out of my life in each area, e.g., what do I want out of my family life?

2. **Why** do I want that? You need to truly understand *why* you want what you want in these areas of your life.

   I suggest you go 7 reasons deep. The first three will be shallow. Keep going. What about the fourth reason and the fifth? Now you're starting to build a meaningful case inside yourself for why these areas need your focus.

3. **How** am I going to get there today?

Using myself as an example again, I ask myself, "Who do I need to be today to make sure I'm tending to the areas that are important to me? Who do I need to be today to make my family understand how much I love them and value them? How am I going to connect today with a fundraising opportunity? How am I going to honor my faith today and connect with my higher power?'

Ask yourself, what are the ways you're going to get there today? How are you going to show up in each of the areas of your life that matter the most to you? Then you'll know where to put your attention.

Now you have something to go by when you ask yourself *Did I Win the Day*? Please understand that doesn't mean you expect to win every day, and that's ok. Having these Daily Focus Areas gives you something to check in with. They let you know where you are, and where you're going.

Focusing on your DFAs steers your attention and helps you put together a day after which you can go to bed and say, *I Won the Day*. Even if you don't achieve a big goal each day, don't give up; maybe it's coming next week or three months from now. The process is about thinking of how to get there and the answer is by focusing on your DFAs each day. They will serve as your blueprint for each day and help you understand that, while you're not going to win big every day, you will be able to see the specific areas in which you didn't win, and plan to focus on them tomorrow.

Every single day is a new opportunity to win.

Focus on the Process.

Win the Day.

Little Kevin. I clearly was not a fan of Santa Claus.

University of Utah Baseball.

My team picture from the Moose Jaw Diamond Dogs.

My girlfriend and I before a game in South Dakota.

My beautiful baby girl KendraJae.

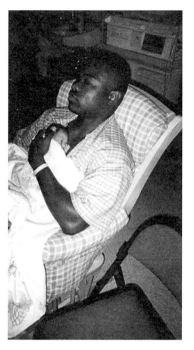
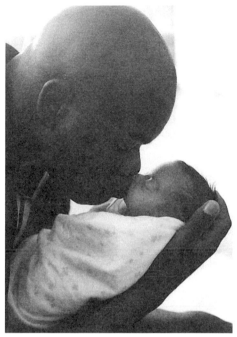

Loving on my baby boy, Kobe J.

Les Brown and I in Atlanta before speaking at T.D. Jake's Mega Fest.

Students of Grant High School galvanizing me at Mile 19 of the California International Marathon

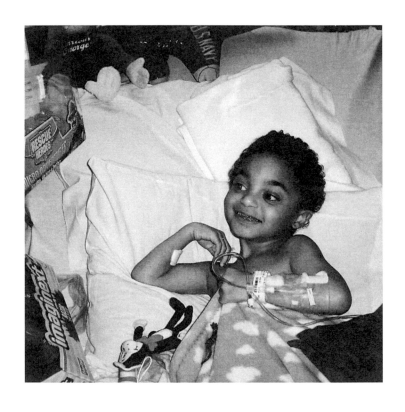

My beautiful baby boy and his trillion dollar smile while in the hospital.

Watsonville High School showed me LOVE.
Ones UP! #EachOneReachOne

Don't miss the message – When your mind goes negative, your mouth goes positive. Photo shoot with TaylorBoone.com

KendraJae living her dream right next to one of the Greatest
entertainers of all time.

Kissing my son after he gave a GREAT speech at my Reach 4 Greatness Show.

MaJa (Momma Jessi) and KendraJae representing.

Reminiscing before a video shoot in front of my childhood duplex. I remember always being scared when I lived here.

My childhood lenses – Sad and Angry

My childhood lenses – Bitter and Confused

My childhood lenses – Hurt and Alone

CHAPTER EIGHT: MAKING A DREAM REAL

Many of us fear the unknown and unexpected. What if you're suddenly forced to make a career change because your company is doing massive layoffs? Or the economy takes a downturn and your small business can't make it? Or the college you always planned on attending turns you down? Or the scholarship offer you were expecting doesn't come through? Or a beloved family member becomes ill and you have to change your plans to care for him or her? Any one of these situations is a prime example of when most people's *scaredness* surfaces in a big way.

And that's ok. Fear is ok. Fear is normal. Fear is human. Fear is an emotion that WILL come up whenever you face an unexpected obstacle to a dream, goal or vision. The question is, how are you going to steer that fear?

The answer lies in how you perceive the situation. Perspective matters! When you can see the obstacle as a detour sign, not a dead end, it becomes an opportunity for Greatness.

All my life growing up, I had a dream of playing professional baseball. I played ball as soon as I was of age to sign up for tee ball and played nonstop through high school. I loved baseball and I saw it as my way forward in life, my path to a better life. I didn't think of doing anything else once I graduated; I didn't think I *needed* to have a 'Plan B.' I had a rock solid 'Plan A' -- or so I thought.

My plan was this -- I was either going to sign a contract to play professionally straight out of high school, or I would get a college scholarship and have the opportunity to play at the Division 1 level during college, after which I'd get drafted and head to the minor leagues and from there to the big leagues.

Unfortunately, my dream hit a detour. When I graduated from high school, nobody offered me a contract and I didn't get the university scholarship I was hoping for. That meant my only chance to play baseball was at a community college, so I rearranged my plan and went to American River College to play baseball and continue my education.

I had never viewed community college as an option until it became my *only* option to play. In my head, I was going to be a star there. American River was not a Division 1 school; therefore, I assumed, the competition wouldn't be as good. Surely, I thought, I was going to show up at American River College and tear that level of baseball apart.

How wrong I was.

When I first walked onto the field to try out, the sheer number of players on the field sent me into my *scared* place. Before I had even laced up my cleats, my mind was racing with doubts: Am I good enough? Am I fast enough? Is my arm strong enough? Will I even make this team?

All the *scared,* all the fear that I lived with came to the surface once again. There were plenty of players that were better than I was and, technically, I did not make the team. It was the last thing I had expected. It felt like a huge defeat.

The 'technical' part was that the coach gave me the option to "red shirt," meaning be a part of the team but not play in games. He wanted me to grow for another year, to get stronger, faster and better. If I did that, I would have another chance to make the team the following year. I wasn't being cut, but man, it sure felt like I was. It felt like a dead end, the end of a dream.

It turned out to be only a detour to my dream. In fact, my red shirt year was the best thing that could have happened for me. It was a year of hard work and dedication that matured me as a player and ultimately propelled me forward on my journey toward playing baseball at the professional level.

I went to school every day and carried a full load of classes. For the first time in my life, I wasn't obligated to be at baseball practice. I had a choice to make -- was I going to keep practicing consistently even though I wasn't 'technically' on the team or was I going to play Nintendo every day after school and spend my free time chasing girls? To be honest, I chose all three.

The thing I did *right* was go to practice every single day. I'd show up for what was called 'early outs' at 1:00 every afternoon, when the red shirts had the chance to practice for an hour before the team hit the field at 2:00. I worked on improving my game for the following year. Because the coach saw me at early outs every day, he knew I was serious about getting better.

Sure, it was embarrassing to my spirit to get redshirted that first year. It was not what I had planned, and it seemed way off track from my dream, but it was exactly what I needed to get better. If it had not been for that detour, I wouldn't have developed the consistency, determination, discipline and work ethic I truly needed to make my average athletic ability pay off.

After three years at American River College, I graduated with an Associate of Arts degree; I did get a scholarship to a Division 1 school, the University of Utah, and I did play pro ball in Canada. Dream achieved!

As I now know, baseball wasn't going to be my only skill set or even my *Best Skill Set*. I discovered my Best Skill Set many years later, after several more detours.

Bracing for Your Best Skill Set

I'm often asked how I discovered my ability, my 'gift' as a professional speaker. To me, this is like being asked, "how do you know when you've found your significant other, the person you want to spend your life with?" The answer is the same to both: You just *know*. You know because you know. There's an internal confirmation that no other human being can validate for you. The answer lies within you.

I discovered my gift only after many years of developing *other* skill sets, of having different dreams at different times and taking many detours along the paths to those dreams. I knew I couldn't play baseball forever, and that was a tough thought. I kept asking myself, "What am I going to do after baseball that will give me the same 'juice' baseball does?" I wanted to find something else that would give me happiness and purpose; I also needed to earn money to support my family.

I knew I loved people and knew I was willing to take a risk, so I got involved in network marketing. It was through that enterprise that I met Ken, my first mentor. As I told you previously, I learned an enormous amount from Ken. Ultimately his mentorship put me on the path to discovering what I call my *Best Skill Set*, not only through the lessons he taught me, but also because he gave me a tape by Les Brown that got stuck in the tape deck of my car.

That tape led me to the epiphany moment I described to you back in Chapter 6. Listening to Les Brown's tape for the thousandth time, I suddenly realized, all he's doing is telling his story and all I have to do is figure out how to tell *mine!*

Once the Les Brown tape made its indelible mark on me, I started accumulating more books and audio programs about speaking. I began to fill my eyes and ears with the stories of people who had achieved success in the field. Eventually I came across the book: *Success Secrets of Motivational Super Stars* by Michael Jeffreys. It gave me insight into the journeys of super successful professional speaking icons like Tony Robbins, Barbara DeAngelis, John Gray, Jack Canfield, Patricia Fripp, Mark Victor Hansen and many others.

I noticed that every single speaker profiled in the book had at least one thing in common -- they all had joined Toastmasters Clubs at the beginning of their journeys. I took that clue and did that too. I joined a Toastmasters Club called River City Speakers.

After my first 'icebreaker speech' at that Toastmasters, I knew what I wanted to do. I had found the thing that made me feel as great as baseball did. Mind you, I wasn't *good* at it yet. But I knew, without a shadow of a doubt, that I wanted to *get good* at speaking because of how I felt after I was done. At first, it wasn't about the audience or the topic or the venue. It was about how I felt after my talks. I felt alive and, almost instantly, I became addicted to that feeling.

Discovering Your Best Skill Set

Not everyone will know what their best gifts are right away, and that's perfectly ok. We can live from our Greatness no matter what. But I want every one of you reading this to be thinking about what your *Best Skill Set* might be because, in order to discover your talents, you need to be seeking them.

Finding what your talents are starts with desire. You don't just stumble into them. You have to be open. You have to be ready. One way to start opening yourself to your possibilities is to ask yourself a lot of questions, like:

- What are my interests?
- What are my strengths?
- What are my hobbies?
- What do I love the most about myself?
- What are my best talents?
- What do I do better than anyone else I know?
- What is something I used to consider a flaw in myself, but now see as an asset?

- What scares me but I still want to do it?
- What would I love to do and get paid for it?

No one can do this for you. Only you can begin the search for your talents, and only you will know when you've found the path you want to begin to explore.

If You Don't Want a Plan B, Get Another Plan A

I could never have predicted the chain of events that led me to discovering my Best Skill Set. Back in high school, I had my dream. I didn't realize there would be other dreams after that, other lessons, other achievements and other discoveries about what I love and what I was capable of.

Fear of the unknown is one of the most common fears people have. When a job ends or a career goes off the rails, the questions about what comes next can create a huge moment of terror. Trust me when I tell you that those moments of fear have the potential to lead you to moments of opportunity if you steer them in the right direction. Even if you can't at first predict where those moments will lead you, embrace them! Trust they will be good guides.

After baseball, I knew I didn't want to get a job that required me to sit in a cubicle. I knew I wouldn't be satisfied going back to a job in social work. In other words, I didn't want a Plan B. The thought of a Plan

114

B was depressing; what I wanted was *another Plan A.*

Today when I speak to athletes, I tell them: "You don't need to have a Plan B, but you *do* need to find something else you're as passionate about as you are about your sport -- not *instead* of your sport but *in addition* to it." Professional athletes can't play forever. Even top-earners who will retire with plenty of money in the bank still need something that gives them 'the juice' for the days ahead, something that feels rewarding and inspiring to focus on and to do.

I get it. You don't even want to *think about* a Plan B. So, don't think of it that way. Think about your next focus points as your other Plan A.

Greatness Leaves Clues

To find your Best Skill Set, you need to be looking for it, you need to open your mind to search for it. When you say, "I don't know what I want to do," your mind isn't open; this is a closed thought, not an open one. There is no curiosity in *I don't know.*

On the other hand, when you say, "I may not be sure at this moment, but I am going to figure out what comes next," then your mind is open.

You must have your antennae up, taking in positive ideas and influences. This is the preparation you need to hear your dream when it speaks to you. You don't always know what will happen, but you won't notice anything if your mind is closed and you don't have any goals. Keep your awareness up by paying attention to what comes into your life, listening to the voice inside and getting a sense of what influences you, what messages resonate with you and what has an impact on you.

It is much easier to keep your antennae up and your mind open if you are staying in a Greatness State of Mind. Use the Gateways that lead to Great Ways by taking in messages that are positive, listening to those who inspire you and spending your time around other people who are positive, forward thinking, chasing their dreams and have interests in common with yours.

As I recommended in Chapter 7, define your DFAs. Check in with yourself and answer the questions: Am I finding joy on the journey? Am I Bettering my Best? Am I staying focused on the process rather than on some end goal in the future?

Use the *Tools for Greatness* to steer your fear of the unknown and unexpected. Yes, you are going to have fear. You are going to have anxiety. You are going to feel nervous about attempting new things. Remember, fear is a part of being alive, and there is power in that fear. One of the purposes of this book is to let you know that you can guide and direct that fear in a powerful way.

Remember, You Won't Be Good at it Right Away

A dream can go completely off the tracks if you *see an obstacle as a dead end*. Another surefire way to derail a dream is to *give up too quickly*. When you find your best talent, your Best Skill Set, you've got to remember, you won't be good at it right away! That's fine! That's why you *Brace Yourself*, why you start with study and preparation. Getting good at it comes later.

I wasn't good at speaking the first time I got up to give a speech, but I kept working at it and I got better. I sharpened my skills through consistent effort. No one just stumbles into Greatness. Greatness is a process, and every part of the process is important, including the struggles, the vulnerable moments and the setbacks. There is value in the moments when you feel like you put yourself out there too much and might get rejected or laughed at. There is value in the moments when you DO get rejected – maybe *especially* in those moments.

If you are showing up and putting it all out there, you are working on finding your Greatness. It won't always feel easy or safe, but persevering will help you get where you want to be. Focus on Winning the Day, not winning the race or winning awards.

How to Make A Dream Real

Brace Yourself
Tools for Greatness
Tool #5: To Make a Dream Real, Do the ROAD WORK

Most performers -- athletes, dancers, gymnasts, musicians, speakers, most performers of every kind – recognize the need to train, to prepare for their performances, to further their careers. Boxers, among others, train using a conditioning exercise consisting of running considerable distances. That exercise is called ROAD WORK and I think it's a perfect model for people seeking their Greatness, trying to make their dreams real.

I believe we all have a dream somewhere within us. It's just that many people have not identified exactly what that dream is yet. If and when that's the case, the first step to making a dream real is to:

1. **DO THE ROAD WORK – IDENTIFY YOUR DREAM**

Be open to new experiences and new information. Make sure you are using the Gateways that lead to Great Ways. Take in positive messages. Carry those messages in your heart and speak them with your mouth. Bring the Best Version of you to every day, no matter whether you are *living the dream* that day or not.

When something unexpected or scary happens, view it as a detour rather than a No Outlet sign. Find joy on the journey, even in the moments when you don't know where that journey is headed. If you haven't discovered your personal dream or your best skill set, identify those facts. Know that it's perfectly ok if that's where you are. Just keep your antennae up and your mind open, and I guarantee you will have your epiphany.

Right now, Identify It.

Write one sentence that encapsulates your dream or goal for now.

2. **DO THE ROAD WORK – PICTURE YOUR DREAM**

This step in the process, picturing your dream, must become as automatic as breathing and blinking. Our minds drift in wonder and amazement all day, every day. We think thousands upon thousands of thoughts per day, and many, if not most, of them are in pictures. We can develop our ability to focus and hold snapshots of those pictures in our minds.

Les Brown says, "Hold the vision." To me, that means to picture your dreams and allow them to surface. When an image of your dream comes up, let it stay there in your mind for a moment. Don't push it away.

Here's another thing Les Brown taught me: "We can't control the thoughts that come to our minds, but we can control the ones we focus on." Start working on this every day. Choose the thoughts you focus on. Visualize what you want rather than what you *don't* want.

What we focus on, we will reproduce. That's true regardless of whether it's positive or negative, whether it's a dream or a nightmare. So be careful what you focus on.

In the early days of my journey to becoming a professional communicator, I pictured myself before audiences of all types. I pictured myself succeeding. I can't even tell you how long I've been picturing this book you're reading.

The more I pictured my dreams, the stronger my desire became to accomplish them. There were times when I became frustrated because I wasn't doing enough work towards my dream to speak or the completion of this book. Those emotions of frustration and pressure are all necessary in the maturation process of going from the inception of an idea to its completion.

Frustration causes us to make things happen. It was frustrating for me to get redshirted my first year at American River College and even more frustrating to sit on the bench the entire year after that as second string second baseman. In fact, I think frustration is necessary to make our dreams reality. Don't let frustration stop you -- let it move you! It's ok to be frustrated, but it's NOT ok to quit!

Visualize yourself having already attained your dream. Visualize yourself going through each of the steps you took to get there. This isn't the same as having a daydream; don't get stuck in picturing just the end goal. Remember the Olympic athletes and their certainty that the process is everything. Focus on visualizing the process to get where you want to go with a positive mindset. Visualize a smooth flow to the process. Begin incorporating this visualization into your day, during your *20 Minutes Alone to Step into Your Greatness Zone*, and when you *End Your Night with Momentum*.

3. **DO THE ROAD WORK – SPEAK IT**
    Nineteen years ago, I identified and pictured what I wanted to do with my life. I began the regimen I told you about in Chapter XX: *20 Minutes Alone to Step into my Greatness Zone*. I started every day with a 20-minute walk, and for five minutes of that walk I would speak out the life I wanted. In Chapter XX, I called these statements *Incantations*; for this chapter I say, *Speak It*.

    As you move about your day trying to find your rhythm in life, make it a point to literally speak out the life you want; put the words into the atmosphere. I think many people choke their dreams by speaking negativity, darkness and death into them without even realizing they're doing it. One of the first ways you can measure your personal growth is by being aware of the words you speak about yourself, about your dreams, and the way you speak to others.

I can usually tell where a person is on his or her journey by having just one conversation with them. People who are making things happen, making an impact and making money are some of the most positive people in the world. You don't very often hear these people beating themselves up with their words, and when they do, they usually notice immediately and correct themselves. They don't let negative language keep them out of alignment with their Greatness.

4. **DO THE ROAD WORK – INK IT**
There is something invigorating about thinking on paper, allowing your writing utensil to slide across the page from one letter to the next, creating words, sentences and paragraphs that

ultimately create meaning for you and hopefully for others. Try it.

I listened to an audio program years ago called *100 Dreams*. The speaker challenged us to "sit and write down 100 Dreams of all the things you'd like to do, be or have in your lifetime. There are no limits, just write." Then the speaker said, "I bet you won't get to 100!"

I am a competitor and I took that as a personal challenge, so I started writing. The speaker was right; I never made it to 100. I did make it to 67 in that first effort; then I picked it back up a few months later, but still never made it to 100.

That was over 17 years ago, and today I have accomplished most of what was on that list, much of it to the letter. I had no idea how magical that simple challenge of writing my dreams would be, and I'm betting, neither do you.

Do you have a writing utensil yet? Get up, get out and go get it! You don't need skill, money or even opportunity to have a dream and write it down. It's imperative to write down what you want. There is almost universal agreement among speakers and authors of personal development messages that it's vital to set goals, write down your goals and put deadlines on them; if you don't, they're not real goals.

I do need to confess that doing that never worked for me. I've never been organized enough to write down the goal, put a date on it and track it hourly, daily, weekly, monthly or quarterly until I reach it. For those who can relate to me, understand that you don't have to do things the *traditional* way all the time to make things happen in your life. However, at some point you DO have to Ink it.

Write your dream down on paper. Take a few minutes and elaborate on your dream. Feel the pen move across the paper as you bring that dream out of the ether and into the real world by putting it down on paper.

5. **DO THE ROAD WORK – STUDY IT**
   A popular marketing angle in today's world is *faster is better*. In some cases that may be true; faster phone service is better, faster Internet is better, faster product delivery is better. But when it comes to chasing a dream, the *faster is better* school of thought doesn't work. It takes time to make your dream a reality. It takes time to learn how to build your business, create your product line, write your book or reach a goal. And it is important to remember that how long it takes to make your dream a reality is directly related to the time it takes to *Study It*.

   I set out to become a professional speaker years ago. I studied almost daily for over 10 years before I saw my business and my brand begin to grow to the level of my goals. I played baseball for over 12 years before my dream to play professionally became a reality. In both cases, those years were spent studying.

For speaking, I read book after book, I listened to audios, old and new, I observed other speakers, wrote down my ideas, cogitated on concepts, created content, I wrote down and asked questions, attended conferences, and gave free speeches to gain experience. All those things fall under the category of studying.

For baseball, I took ground balls, hit batting practice, played catch, worked out and talked with others who were further along than I was. All that falls under the category of studying, too.

I live my dream today because of 2 things, discipline and studying. I invested time and prepared myself for the experiences and opportunities that I'm now faced with in my speaking life. And because I'm still *scared* to this day, every time I step on stage

I'm prepared. I have prepared by studying.

Malcom Gladwell, in his book, *Outliers,* talks about how 10,000 hours of deliberate practice are needed to become world-class in any field. What hour of deliberate practice would you estimate you are on? Just asking.

To focus on what and how to study, make a list of ways you can start doing this. If you're searching for your best skill set, what tools can you use to keep your mind open? Would it help for you to listen to motivational speakers or great podcasts in the car? How about going to events you wouldn't normally go to?

If you have a specific goal, what can you do to start studying that craft? What books are you going to look for and read? What classes will you sign up for at the local community college? What lectures, talks or conferences will you attend?

Commit yourself to the course of study you need to show yourself approved.

6. DO THE ROAD WORK – GET AROUND IT

You may dream globally but focus (start) locally. To achieve any dream that involves a professional, creative, artistic or career goal, you need to get into the world where that thing is happening. If your dream is to become an actor on Broadway, you need to start by getting your feet onto a stage somewhere. You need to be spending time in theaters, at whatever level you can right now.

I'm not saying, if acting on Broadway is your dream, you should pack up and move to New York today. I'm suggesting that you start by getting involved in whatever type of theater you can. Maybe that means going to a meeting of the drama club at your school, or auditioning for a community theater production of *Peter Pan* or being an extra on a film being shot near where you live. All of these are ways of *getting around it*, even if you don't have much experience yet. By *getting around it*, you start making connections with people who are in the world you want to be a part of. You create opportunities for yourself to learn what you need to know and to meet the people who can teach you or propel you forward on your path.

When I first realized I wanted to tell my story and inspire others as a professional speaker, I had no connections whatsoever in the world of speaking. How was I going to live my dream if I didn't start getting into that world? I had to start somewhere, so I joined the local Toastmasters club. That decision launched my journey; it propelled me forward to the next steps as my connections grew, leading me to more teachers, mentors and opportunities.

> What club, what organization,
> what group of people locally are
> doing what you want to do?
> When do they meet? Where do
> they meet? How often do they
> meet? Go get are around them!

I remember receiving an email in the late 1990s that Les Brown was going to be speaking at a church in Oakland, California. Initially fear rose up inside of me, fear of failure -- fear that I would not achieve my goal to meet him face to face -- fear that others would have the same idea I did which would mess up my 'master plan.'

On the other hand, a child-like excitement surfaced inside of me as well. I had been listening to this man's voice on tapes, reading his books and studying his VHS (remember those? Some do, some don't) videos...*and now* he was about to be in Oakland, just *72 miles from my door step!*

That email kept me up all night, my emotions weaving in and out between fear and excitement. I tossed and turned, trying to visualize a scenario where I could separate myself from everybody else to get a moment alone with Les.

I had to do something with these emotions, so I jumped out of bed and poured my thoughts out to him in a letter.

The next morning my best friend Jason Hamilton and I drove to Oakland; when we arrived, I immediately started thinking about ways to get back stage to meet the man I dearly hoped would be my future mentor. As we approached the entrance, we were told, "Mr. Brown's almost done with the first service, so wait here and when the second service starts, you'll be among the first to get in."

We waited and as we stood there, I thought to myself, *this scenario is not going to get me what I want,* so I walked around to the back of the church. It was blocked off with yellow caution tape which told me I probably was somewhere I was not supposed to be. I snuck around the tape, tested a couple of doors that were locked and kept trying until I found one that was unlocked allowing me to open it. I almost passed out! I was light headed; my heart was beating out of my chest.

I knew I wasn't supposed to be back there, but I was on a mission. This was my chance to meet the only person who was doing what I wanted to do, at the level at which I wanted to do it. I had studied him and now I was *respectfully* pursuing him.

I found myself standing in an empty room, sweating profusely, my whole body jolting with every heartbeat. I had my letter in one hand, a VHS video recording of a speech I gave at CSU East Bay in my other and a determined spirit flooding my body. All of a sudden, I heard thunderous applause on the other side of the wall, signaling that Les was concluding his first service. Next thing I knew, I looked to my left and in walked Les Calvin Brown.

I was face to face with the Motivational Legend I idolized, mimicked and listened to daily, the man whose footsteps I wanted to follow to a tee. His first words were, "how did you get back here?"

I replied, "I snuck back here, Mr. Brown, I watch all your videos, listen to all of your tapes and have read your books. You're doing what I want to do, Mr. Brown; you've helped me raise my opinion of myself; and I hope you will help me even more. I don't want you to do anything for me except please give me some knowledge and wisdom about how to do this. I want to touch lives in the way you touch lives." As I slipped my letter to him into his shirt pocket, I went on to say, "I wrote you a letter and brought a video of me speaking that I hope you will watch." I handed him the video and he just stood there and looked at me. It was an uncomfortable pause, then he looked right in my eyes and said, "Son, go sit in the front row because, after I'm done speaking today, you and I have some business to take care of."

I was thrilled! I went back into the church to find my buddy. There was no room on the front row, so we stood in the back. Les stepped on stage and began to speak. His words shocked me.

He said, "ladies and gentlemen, before I get started, I'd like to acknowledge a young man. This young man came from Sacramento to hear me speak. He came back stage -- no one is supposed to be back stage. Security, are you doing your job?" he said jokingly. "This young man had an energy, had a boldness, an excitement about himself that's the kind of boldness you gotta have when you're chasing a dream. Ladies and gentlemen that's Kevin Bracy. Kevin wave so everybody can see your face please." So I stepped out and gave a Miss America wave like it was my show.

After that day, I thought my life was about to change forever. Well, it didn't – not immediately! I had to keep grinding and grinding for a few years before I joined Les Brown's Speakers' Network which then created an opportunity to share a stage with him in Kansas City.

What that chance, that opportunity, did for me was confirm that I was on the right road, in the right lane of my purpose on earth. All the things that lined up on that day for me to be face to face with Les were orchestrated by God.

I had found someone doing what I wanted to do at the level at which I wanted to do it, studied him and respectfully, yet boldly, pursued him.

7. **DO THE ROAD WORK – FIND SOMEONE DOING IT / FIND A MENTOR**

Find someone doing what you want to do at the level at which you want to do it. Study that person; respectfully pursue the person so you can find ways to:

Learn from him or her

Serve him or her and/or his or her cause, mission or business

Partner with him or her to position yourself to learn all you can

8. **DO THE ROAD WORK – DON'T STOP – GET IT! GET IT!**

This step is self-explanatory. As the late, great Jim Valvano of the Jimmy V Foundation said, "Don't Give Up...Don't Ever Give Up!"

Develop your Game Plan and Identify it. Picture it. Speak it. Ink it. Study it. Get Around it. Find Someone Doing It. Don't Stop - Get It! Get It!

These tools, these steps may seem minute and insignificant when you are impatient to reach a goal. Believe me, I get it. I'm one of the most impatient people I know. But the truth is, these daily habits are some of the most powerful tools we have. And doing them does not require money, opportunity, mentorship, or even talent. The only question is: Will you do it?

CHAPTER NINE: WHAT YOU FOCUS ON, YOU REPRODUCE

On December 23, 2003, I had just gotten off a plane in Seattle, where I would be speaking at a couple of high schools. I switched my phone back on and there was a short but excited voicemail from my wife, Jessica. She said, "Go check Les Brown's website as soon as you can." I knew from her tone that something serious was up. I couldn't wait to get to a computer.

At this point, I had been speaking for over five years. I was loving it, but I was also feeling antsy and ready to go to the next level. I didn't know what the next level looked like, but I did know there was no going back. Les Brown had already influenced me irreversibly. There was no way I would be able to return to an office job or social work. I had become 'psychologically unemployable,' meaning I was no longer thinking like a 9 to 5 employee. It literally made me sick to my stomach to even think about going back to a job.

Les had already inspired me so much to live my dream as a speaker that I had burned those bridges behind me. There was no going back, only forward. I knew that, in order to get to the next level, I was going to have to get around someone who was already there and could mentor me to that space. I had never really thought Les Brown would be that person, but my wife's phone call gave me the impression it was possible.

As soon as I got to my friend JC's house, I got on the computer and went to Les Brown's website. He was marketing a Les Brown Speakers Network with options to join at various levels of investment: $1,000, $2,500, $5,000 or $10,000. I instantly knew I needed to take advantage of this opportunity, but it certainly didn't look as if it would be easy. Money was a huge issue, but I knew I couldn't let that stop me.

Thankfully, I am blessed in my marriage. Jessica is not only brilliant and funny, she also has a mindset of optimism and faith. And she's prudent. Jessica knew as well as I did that investing in this opportunity was a chance we needed to take if we were going to reach our goals of financial stability. Together, we figured out a way to do it. We sold some of our belongings, emptied our savings account and got a loan from Jess's father, Sammy J. Cohen, who had always been and one of my main mentors, to cover the rest. Then we put down it all down on the Les Brown Speakers Network.

Talk about a SCARED GREAT moment! I was investing pretty much everything we had as a family on this one chance. Could I live up to this investment and my wife's faith in me? My heart was in my mouth, but I *knew* I had to do it. I had to take the chance in order to broaden my sphere of opportunity. I was scared, but I knew, deep down, it would pay off in some kind of way.

The first two months after joining the network brought total stagnation. There was absolutely nothing, not a single phone call to offer a speaking date. As you can imagine, I jumped a little every time the phone rang. I would not let myself get discouraged; I just knew one of those days I would get the call I was waiting for.

Finally, on February 4, 2004, that's exactly what happened. I was invited to share the stage with Les Brown in Kansas City for an event that was scheduled for February 22.

Needless to say, I spent the next two and a half weeks in full-on Brace Mode, preparing for what I knew was the opportunity of a lifetime. There were two things that would make or break my dream to make a living as a professional speaker -- how I did on that stage in Kansas City and what Les Brown thought of me.

What You Focus on the Longest Becomes the Strongest

Flying into Kansas City, I had crazy butterflies in my stomach. I was charged with mixed feelings of excitement, anticipation, disbelief and of course FEAR.

I got off the plane and walked to curbside where I was met by a limousine. When the driver got out to open the door, I heard Les's booming voice. He was on a phone call inside the limo. As I got in, Les continued his phone call but, at the same time, looked me up and down, checking out my suit and gaining his first impression of me. I was *SCARED*, but I was also *PREPARED*. I had made sure that my appearance was top-notch, and I could tell that Les was impressed.

He finished his phone call and gave me the rundown of events for the next two days. We would be sharing the stage at an event called, "Bringing Out the Millionaire in You." I was so far from a millionaire that the name alone scared the heck out of me! I would have felt like a total fraud speaking on that topic, except I had read so many books written by millionaires that I *could think like one*. I was prepared.

After the first seminar, Les called me in my hotel room at a little after midnight. He said, "Kevin, you are ready. I could give you $20,000 worth of speaking engagements right now and you'd be prepared for them. Your stage presence, your presence of mind, your body language, your ability to remember quotes and tell stories are all phenomenal. You remind me of the hunger for speaking I had when I first began."

I did another seminar with Les and then we hit the road, I barely spent any time at home for the next year and a half. I was literally learning on the move, going from engagement to engagement. It was my apprenticeship, and I was being mentored by the best in the business.

How had I gotten to this level? I know I attracted that opportunity through hard work and the grace of God. How I responded to the opportunity was up to me. I first had to make a commitment via an investment, then I had to be patient, then I had to be prepared.

Les Brown's mentorship changed the whole trajectory of my life. Today, all these years later, I make an incredible living as a professional speaker due in very large part to the things I learned from him in that year and a half.

I am that I SAY I am.
Not everyone will have the same experience I had of meeting their hero and then partnering with that person and being mentored by him or her. I know that. The point is that what you *focus on, you will become*, eventually, one way or another, for better *or* for worse.

I am that I SAY I am. *You* are what you SAY you are. You are what you speak about yourself and what you speak about your life. When you attend to your words with the right energy, the words you speak both to yourself and to others will help you attract the opportunities you seek. You have the ability to be in the world you want to be in. You have the ability to attract the teachers, collaborators and mentors who will help you take your journey to the places you dream of.

I truly believe that the combination of God's grace over my life, coupled with my imagination of who I wanted to become and the WORDS I attended to via the Gateways that Lead to Great Ways are the reasons for where I am today in my life.

I am that I SEE I am.
You are what you take in. You are the words you speak. And, you are what you SEE yourself as.

I am that I SEE I am. After I got that pit bull grip on my dream to become a professional speaker, it was still going to be a long time before I could quit my day job. I still had a job in social work, as a counselor, but I held the vision of myself in my mind as a professional speaker.

I began to dress, think and behave for the career that was my dream, being a motivational speaker. It didn't hurt my day job at all. In fact, it made me more effective in working with clients. The more I began to SEE myself as an inspiring and positive person, the more inspiring I became. That's because what you focus on, you will become.

I am that I SEE I am.

I am that I THINK I am.
One day after a speaking engagement with Les and a few other speakers, we all joined Les and his daughter, Ona Brown, for dinner. I admire Ona Brown for many reasons including her unmatched oratorical brilliance, but the single thing I'll always most appreciate her for is what she said to me that day. During a private moment at dinner, Ona turned to me and asked bluntly, "Kevin, do you think you're fine?"

I was a little thrown off by how direct her question was. I had to think about it for a minute and as I write this, I can't remember how I responded.

Ona could see I was struggling and came to my rescue with a quick follow-up question: "*When* do you think you're fine?"

I answered honestly, "I think I'm fine when I'm clean shaven, dressed up in a suit like right now, when my head is freshly shaved." I rattled off some other things.

Ona, thrown off by my answer, shook her head and said, "You need to be like Johnny." She was speaking of my great friend and Worldwide Speaker/Entrepreneur Johnny Wimbrey. "He *knows* he's fine, so when he gets on stage, he owns it!"

She continued, "You're fine in a suit, in your sweats, whether you're clean shaven or not, whether you're ashy or not. You are fine all the time and you need to own that all the time. When you do, it will carry over to you owning the stage."

I was around 33 when Ona Brown uttered these words to me. I had already spent years re-programming my self-image through positive thinking and developing a Muhammad Ali mindset. I was speaking self-confidence into myself every day, building myself up. I had come a long way from the insecurities and self-capping I picked up in my scared childhood.

But Ona saw something else, too, and in that moment, I felt she was seeing right through me. My view of myself still depended on other things, like my appearance and clothes. Her words shifted the vision I had of myself. She made me look at something deeper -- self-acceptance. Knowing and owning who I am no matter what. After that day, I walked a little taller, spoke a little more authoritatively and had a permanent swagger increase all because of how my view of myself had changed.

When you accept yourself on a bad day just as much as you do on a good day, you are going to radiate confidence. You will look fine, sound fine, and inspire the people around you no matter what you're wearing or what your hair looks like or whether or not you even have hair (I don't).

Because you ARE that you THINK you are.

I am that I DO.
Ultimately, I AM that I DO. The actions we take define us. When my words are in alignment with my visions, and my thoughts are in alignment with my words, it becomes almost effortless that what I DO will be in alignment with my dreams.

What are you DOING now? Are you taking the steps to BE the person you want to be? Are you taking Right Actions towards your dreams?

What does it take to make a dream real? Identify it. Ink it. Picture it. Speak it. Study it. Get Around it. Find Someone Doing It. Don't stop, Get It Get It.

Every one of these things is an action. You ARE that you DO. Guide and direct your fear into taking the actions you need to take. Brace yourself with preparation.

You ARE that you DO.

Right Focus, Right Intention, Right Action

It is often suggested that the beginning of depression is wrong thinking. 'Wrong thinking' means thinking and dwelling on past situations or future scenarios. If you dwell too much in the past, you're thinking about things that have already happened and that you can't change now. As for worrying about the future, what good is it to imagine negative scenarios or outcomes that haven't happened yet and may never happen? That's nothing but a waste of energy.

Dwelling on the past and worrying about the future keep you from being right here, right now. None of us has much control over the past or the future. What *do* you have control over? Right here, right now. That's it. What are you going to do right now, in this moment? That's a choice you *can* make. That's a place where you *do* have power.

Staying in the present is staying in your *Right Mind*. If you live your life actively every day, bringing your Right Focus, Right Thinking and Right Intention to what you do, you will have a consistent source of positive energy and motivation. You will look for reasons to be motivated rather than reasons to be discouraged.

Fuel Your Motivation

The human body needs to be fed with carbs, proteins, water and other nutrients in order to function at its highest level of efficiency and longevity. To sustain your body long-term, you have to feed it the right things.

Motivation is just like the human body. In order to be effective and long-lasting, motivation must be fed every single day. If a day goes by that you don't feed your motivation in some way, it will surely wane. You can count on that.

How do you feed your motivation? It begins with the words you give attention to and the words you speak into yourself. Words and phrases like 'I can't, I'll never, I'm not good enough, I'm a loser, I'm dumb,' are like poison to your mind, your motivation, and your journey to your Greatness.

If you want your motivation to thrive, stay healthy and give you energy on your journey, you will give your attention to the right words -- words like: "I can, it's doable, it's possible, I can dream, I am a winner, I am brilliant, I am positive, I will do it, I don't give up on my Greatness." Feeding these words into yourself is like feeding your body a healthy, nutrient-rich diet. They give you the energy and stamina to win the day and do the work to make your dreams a reality, every day.

A few years back, I attended a Kanye West concert in my hometown of Sacramento. I happened to be in a state of mind where I wasn't really believing in my vision, my talent or my gifts. I was still working towards my dream, trying my best to stay motivated, but I was losing my mojo and it felt like I was a long way from where I wanted to be. My belief in myself wasn't where it needed to be to take the right actions.

I got a call from a friend who had an extra ticket to see Kanye and Rihanna who was opening the show. I hadn't planned on going but I followed my intuition that maybe I could find some juice from this concert, so I took my friend up on the offer. I went to the concert looking for a reason to be motivated. I let myself be open to the experience, to anything that would clear my vision and increase my confidence.

Watching Rihanna and Kanye West perform fueled my motivation. Their amazing performances helped me find the inspiration I needed to keep moving forward, to keep thinking Right Thoughts and taking Right Action towards my dreams.

That night, Kanye passed out a small book to every person in the crowd. I was so inspired by the style and design of the book that I went home and started writing a little book of my own. That concert was the impetus behind my youth book called, *Greatness Leaves Clues.* It was just one stepping stone on the way to the book you're reading now, which would not exist if I had not found a way to keep my motivation fueled.

You can look either for reasons to keep moving forward or reasons to stop you from moving forward. Although I had been in a negative state of mind that day before my friend called, I went to the show looking for reasons to have a breakthrough. I found what I was looking for. We usually do. If I had gone to that show looking for a reason to be discouraged, to feel envious or 'not good enough,' or 'not talented' enough, I could have found that too.

Look for a reason to stay motivated, in every day and every moment of your day. Be open. Whatever you focus on the longest becomes the strongest. Whatever you give the most attention to will become your strongest desire. If you're looking for reasons to be angry or jealous or depressed, I guarantee you will find them. And, if you're looking for inspiration and motivation, you will find them just about everywhere.

You are that you SAY You Are. You are that you SEE you are. You are that you THINK you are. You are that you DO.

Brace Yourself
Tools for Greatness
Tool #6: Stay in Your Right Mind

Start with you.

Focus your attention on your gifts.

Return to Chapter 4 and check out your Greatness Statements if you need to.

Check in: are you maintaining a Greatness Mindset?

Write out the answers to these questions, the next time your mind goes negative, use your answers to make your mind go positive.

> What do *you* love the most about you?
>
> What are your best talents?
>
> What do you do better than anyone else you know?
>
> What is something about yourself you used to consider a flaw, but now see as an asset?

Now, look outside yourself. Where do you find your motivation fuel?

> Is it going to concerts? Going to the gym? Running in the morning? Reading a book a week? Reading articles or

watching films/podcasts/audio
books from people you admire?
People who inspire you and give
you positive energy?

Make a list of some motivational fuel
you can start taking in right now.

Say YES to invitations instead of NO.
Seek out the things that inspire you.
Remember your motivation needs
fuel, just as your body needs food.

CHAPTER TEN: THE WORD IS "PASSIOUSNESS"

How do you know when you're being presented with an opportunity for Greatness?

You know because you feel *scared*, yet excited. You feel nervous yet have the longing and desire to achieve anyway. My daughter, Kendra Jae, has made up a word for that feeling; it's *'passiousness,'* the special combination of *passion* and *nervousness* that fills you when you're about to do something that really matters to you, when you have a chance to step into your Greatness. You are excited beyond belief, and, at the same time, you are terrified beyond belief because you don't want to fail.

'Passiousness' feels like butterflies in the stomach. It feels like part of you wants to run away but another part of you is absolutely charged with the energy to stay and follow through. That's because the things that matter most are often also the things that scare you.

Kendra Jae came up with the word *'passious'* when she was about 10 years old. Ever since she was little, all she had ever wanted to do was dance. She did gymnastics and played basketball, and she was good at those things, but they didn't hold her interest the way dancing did. The moment she discovered dance

153

she found the thing that held her interest. Through jazz, ballet, hip hop and tap classes as a little girl she found her passion and has never let it go.

She practiced every day. She went to conventions and competitions. At a particularly memorable convention in San Jose, California, she 'killed it,' winning several awards, one of which was professional representation by a talent agency. The agency began setting her up with all kinds of auditions that launched the first phase of Kendra's career as a performer.

We lived in Northern California at that time, and suddenly Kendra was represented by an agency in Southern California. Most of her auditions were five hours away from our home. When the talent agency would call with a commercial or TV show audition they had set up for her, we -- either my wife or I, or Kendra's mom or her mom's husband -- would take turns getting her to these auditions. All of us were encouraging of Kendra's dream, but I must admit, I felt I really related to it in a special way.

I believe in dreaming big. I did then and I still do. I understood where Kendra was coming from with her big dreams, so I volunteered to be the one driving her most often. As we drove from Northern to Southern California and back over those years, we developed a very sweet relationship, talking and singing for hours at a time.

One day, on the way to an audition, she said, "Dad, I'm really nervous." I could tell from the way she said it that her *scared* was surfacing, and she was struggling with it. I said, "I understand that; it makes sense. You know, a lot of people think when they're nervous they're doing something wrong. But you're not. Right now, you're nervous because you have passion for something. The passion says, '*I want to do this.*' The nerves come from '*I don't want to fail.*' The only reason you feel both of those feelings is because you care about how you do. And that's a good thing, not a bad thing."

In that moment, Kendra came up with her own word. She said, "I'm passious, then." Passionate and nervous. Nervousness and passion. Passiousness. That became our word and she would let me know whenever she felt it.

Kendra continued to dance. As a child, she performed on several commercials and in a show for kids called *Hip-Hop Harry*, kind of like the hip-hop version of *Sesame Street.* When she was a teenager, she didn't want to go to college. After she graduated from high school, she came downstairs one night and said, "Dad, I want to move to L.A." We all talked about it, worked it out, and that's what she did.

That was in 2012. That year and the year after, Kendra went to audition after audition after audition and got rejection after rejection after rejection. It turned out that, as a young woman, it was much harder to land those jobs than it had been as a child.

But she didn't give up. She went to audition after audition after audition. She got rejection after rejection after rejection. Audition after audition after audition. NO after NO after NO.

2014 and 2015: Audition after audition after audition. NO after NO after NO.

She lost her representation at the end of 2015; because she wasn't getting any work, the agency dropped her. She knew, if she had told us, we were likely to say it might be time to come home, so she didn't say anything; she just kept working. And kept going to auditions.

2016: January auditions, NO, February auditions, NO. March auditions, NO.

For three years and three months, all she heard was NO. She worked three jobs to pay her bills and keep her apartment. At the same time, she went to every audition she could, but got not one single booking in all that time.

She continued her education. She got a scholarship to the Debbie Reynolds School of Dance where she worked on improving her craft. She took jazz, tap, hip-hop, African dance, ballet and heels classes. She continued working, working out and auditioning every chance she got.

At class one day, a girl said to her casually, "Hey, did you hear about the Beyoncé audition later today?" Having no agent, Kendra had not heard about it. She knew that crashing an audition without representation goes against the dance/audition world protocol; nonetheless, that's exactly what she did.

She walked into that audition alone. She looked around. She was surrounded by countless beautiful, talented young women who had all been invited by their agents. She was not even supposed to be there.

Talk about *Scared Great...* Kendra was terrified. She was shaking. She was full of that feeling we always talked about, the name of which she had invented. She was full of *passiousness*.

When she told me the story later, she said, "Dad, I just decided right then: I am going to go ALL OUT. I don't care who's around, who's looking, who's judging. I'm going to leave it all out on the dance floor." And that's what she did...and she got a call back for a second audition!

And then another call back. And another. And another, until finally, after three and a half years of auditions, she got her first YES. She was hired to be a dancer on the *Formation Tour* with Beyoncé, one of the greatest entertainers of all time.

That one YES has opened a deluge of opportunities. I can't keep track of all she's being offered and all she's doing. I do know I'm not sending her money anymore, but, of course, that's not what matters to me. What I'm proud of is that she never gave up; she created her own life and is living her dream as a professional dancer just like she said she would. Even as I edit this chapter, Kendra Jae is about to embark as one of 6 dancers on the European leg of a tour with the rapper Drake.

All because she danced TOWARD that *passious* feeling, never away from it. The message she taught me is, "It's not about how big you can dream, it's about how long you can dream big."

Get Around the Passiousness

The first time I got up in front of the River City Toastmasters group to give a four-minute speech, my hands were sweating, and my heart was racing. I was hyper-aware of every eye in the room watching me. I had spent the previous week preparing for this short speech. The thought of giving it had made me feel like I was going to die. It was terrifying.

To an outsider, that might look like a low-stakes event. There was no money on the table, no job on the line. If I didn't speak like a pro and captivate everyone in the room, it would not mean losing a contract, a record deal or an opportunity of a lifetime. It would not jeopardize my bank balance and it wouldn't be the end of my business. It wouldn't even mean losing the respect of the people in the room. In fact, it would be understandable if I flopped. After all, it was the first time in my life I had ever given a speech in front of an audience. It was completely voluntary, a short introductory speech to a group of amateur speakers like me, people from various walks of life who were interested in cultivating their speaking skills for various reasons. It didn't have to be mind-blowing.

But to me, it felt like the bottom of the 9th inning, a runner on 2nd and 3rd with two outs, and I was stepping up to the plate. It felt like it mattered. After my speech, I felt as if I had just delivered a double, scoring the go-ahead runs leading to a team victory. That was the moment I really *identified my Dream*. Speaking was going to be the thing that would lead me to my Greatness.

Was my speech good? No, not particularly. Everybody applauded and several people gave me compliments afterward, but they weren't really praising the speech itself or even my skill. They just perceived that I had a passion for it. Some of them saw the potential I had, but they didn't see me give a life-changing speech that day. I took in the praise and at the same time I knew the truth; I had a million things to learn, a million ways to improve.

Nonetheless, I was ELATED. I had just discovered my dream. I immediately got a pit bull grip on that dream. I locked my jaws around it and knew I would never let it go unless I ran out of breath. I thought, "This is what I am going to do for the rest of my life."

All because I went TOWARD that passious feeling, not AWAY from it.

'It's Doable' Is a Frame of Mind

The 'It's Doable' mindset applies to anything you can think of -- starting your own business, getting your degree, writing your book, pioneering a new concept. The perspective is *If it's been done before by anyone at any time, then it's doable for you.*

As you already know, in high school I had a dream of playing professional baseball. I wanted to get a baseball scholarship but didn't know if it was realistic to think that was possible. After someone from my high school got a full ride scholarship for track to the University of Texas, my perspective shifted. That person's example gave me hope that I could get an athletic scholarship too.

It's Doable. If someone has done it somewhere, sometime, then you can too. And what if it *hasn't* been done before? Well, it's still doable for you. After all, anything that's ever been done had to be done for the first time by someone. And that someone could be you. You could be the pioneer for that concept or idea. You could *become* the prototype, motivating someone else one day to believe that It's Doable for them.

There's always a first. Why not you? Why not now?

Russell Simmons was the first entrepreneur I knew to package a comedy show that created a platform for up-and-coming comedians to display their gifts. He then expanded his Def Jam brand, thereby creating a platform for poets to share their truth through poetry.

His vision for those television shows highlighting comedy and poetry became the frame of reference for me to do the same thing. I created a live show highlighting motivational speaking; I conceived it as a platform for positive messages to be delivered by a new generation of motivational superstars. It started off as an idea in my head as I watched Russell Simmons; today we have 10 shows in the can, 10 productions of *Kevin Bracy's MonSTARS of*

Motivation. That kind of show had never been done before in the motivational industry. I wouldn't have moved toward making my vision real if I hadn't believed it could be done.

Whether it has or has not been done before, *It's Doable* for you. It all depends on your mindset.

CHAPTER ELEVEN: IN A SCARED GREAT MOMENT

Do you have to believe it to achieve it? Can you still succeed when you're overwhelmed and gripped by fear?

It was December 5, 2011 and I was on the verge of running my first marathon. At the starting line of the California International Marathon amid 9,000 runners, I felt like the only person there who didn't have the ability to do this thing. I reflected back to the 36-plus miles I had run to prepare for this day. I had been training for three months, but the 26.2 miles ahead of me still seemed impossible. I was gripped by fear and self-doubt.

BANG! As the gun went off and 9,000 runners took that first step, I drew in a deep breath and said to myself, "Here we go!" There was nothing in my mind, body or soul that assured me I could complete what I had prepared so hard for. I had no belief at all that I would reach the finish line. In that moment, I just decided I would run until I passed out. I thought that would be the best I could do, so I would do that much. There was no way I could imagine this ended with me not passing out somewhere along the line; I was sure of that.

I put one foot in front of the other; I continued to take deep breaths. As I approached mile 6, a group of about 30 students from Grant High School were there to cheer me on. They held up signs saying, "Brace Yourself!" and yelled, "You can do it, Kevin! We believe in you!" Their encouragement made me want to cry, but I couldn't because that would have been a waste of energy – *and of* hydration. I needed every ounce of both if I was going to keep going.

I didn't believe in myself. I didn't think I could finish what was ahead of me, but seeing the students gave me a surge of strength. I was running to raise funds for their school. I was running for *them*, and their belief in me helped me believe that I could keep going.

As I approached mile 9, my biggest nightmare became a reality. My calves began to cramp up, my hamstrings began to tighten and fear began to overwhelm me. I wanted to give up. I wanted to slow down and start walking, but just then I looked over to my right. My running coach, Jason Harper, was running next to me, matching me stride for stride. My pride wouldn't allow me to slow down and walk now so I kept going.

"How you doing?" my coach asked. I couldn't even reply, I was so out of breath and nearly in full-panic mode. He must have seen the answer in my face. "Did you see those kids at mile 6?" he asked. I nodded. "Yes!" "Ninety-five percent of their fathers may have quit on them," he said. "Ninety-five percent of the men in their lives may have quit on them."

That was enough to make me stand up a little bit taller. The pressure of those words shot through me as a surge of motivation. I was doing this for a reason, and he had just reminded me of that.

A moment later, I saw a bus driving towards us on the left side of the street. *What the heck is a bus doing on the trail?* I thought. As the bus approached us, my mentor asked, "Do you see that bus?" "How could I miss it?" I gasped, out of breath. "That's the bus for the quitters," he said. "Do you want me to stop it for you?"

Another surge of motivation shot through me. He was playing mind games with me because he knew the word 'quit' is not even in my lexicon; it's not in my vocabulary; it is not in my language.

I stood a little taller, found some breath from somewhere, and kept running. I resisted the urge to walk. J. Harp's words had just the effect he was going for. I was frustrated and annoyed to hear - or even think - the word 'quitter' in reference to myself. I was more determined than ever not to slow down, not to give up. Next thing I knew, he had veered off to go help someone else.

I was approaching mile 13 when I saw the same students cheering for me again, seven miles later. They kept cheering me on, keeping me going with the energy of their belief in me. I got to mile 16, 17, 18. At mile 19, they were waiting for me again and ran about a quarter of a mile with me to inspire me.

Five hours and 10 minutes later, I was finishing something I had absolutely no belief I could finish, something that gripped me with fear. I finished something I did not believe I could do.

So again, I ask you, do you have to believe it to achieve it? Can you still succeed when you're overwhelmed and gripped by fear? The answer to both those questions is YES, absolutely.

You Can *Achieve* Without *Belief*

How many times have you heard something like this: "You've just got to believe in yourself; If you believe in yourself, you can do anything." "Whatever the mind can conceive or believe, it can achieve." (Napoleon Hill)

I talk to young kids all the time and I know they hear this message from teachers and parents. On the surface it's hard to argue with. However, I am here to do just that. I respectfully disagree that you have to *believe* it in order to *achieve it.*

Imagine you're a kid like I was, growing up with little money, sometimes hungry, scared all the time, listening to your parents fight. Imagine looking around for positive reinforcement and encouragement but instead of being ignored or possibly worse, insulted and beaten down, because the adults in your life are struggling so much. Imagine how hard it is to just *believe in yourself* when you don't see the adults around you believing in themselves.

What if the adults in your life actively tell you they *don't* believe in you? What if they tell you you're going to fail? What if they tell you not to expect much out of life because things didn't go well for them? Maybe you don't have to imagine it because you have already lived this experience. Either way you can see how, in that context, it would be pretty tough to just *decide* to believe in yourself.

But that *does not* mean you can't achieve.

Yes, it is important to keep your mind and your words positive. It's important to speak your dreams into being. And it's important to visualize what you want rather than what you don't want. Does lack of belief in yourself or your ability necessarily mean you will not achieve? Of course not.

We can never know for sure if we will achieve something until *after* that moment has come and gone. Anyone who tells you there are guarantees in life, or that confidence and belief alone can determine a positive outcome, is trying to sell you something and you should be suspicious.

It is unreasonable to expect yourself or others to have so much belief or confidence that *fear* will disappear. Fear is going to be there. Self-doubt is going to come up. The fear of failing is going to breathe down your neck sometimes. You can't make that go away for good.

What you CAN focus on is accepting and embracing that fear. You can prepare yourself for the challenges that you will face and that you choose to take on. You can control your level of preparation. You can achieve, even when you are full of fear. Brace Yourself. You can achieve, even when you don't believe you can.

What does it take to achieve when you have no belief that you can? What does it take to achieve when you are gripped by *scared*?

My marathon story is an example. Here's the breakdown, the elements of how I achieved on that particular day, even though, I promise you, I had NO belief that I would. The 'how to' looked like this:

- **Preparation:** I prepared for 90 days by running 360 miles prior to stepping up to the starting line.

- **Game Plan:** I had a game plan. I fueled my body with water and calories every 15 minutes. Even when I could barely keep going, I stuck to the game plan. I kept running. My game plan included 'keep running until you pass out'—somehow, I never passed out.

- **A Reason:** When you're in pursuit of something you truly care about, your reason will drive you through the fear. It will even drive you through the lack of belief in yourself. My reason that day was to raise money for a sports Health Academy to be built at Grant High School. The students cheering me on were my reason. I thought of them the whole time and that reason kept pushing me forward.

- **CIP, *Consistent Infinitesimal Progression*:** When you're gripped by fear, just focus on the baby steps. Even tiny baby steps towards your goal mean you are still progressing. You are moving forward. Don't think about the end result; just keep moving. In the marathon, I just kept moving forward, no matter how much I wanted to stop. As my coach would often tell me, "*Forward is fast.*"

- **A Coach:** I don't know if I would have reached the finish line that day if J. Harp hadn't shown up to reframe my thinking. He reminded me to think about something even deeper than the fact that those kids cheering me on needed a sports Health Academy, the fact that maybe other men in these kids' lives had failed them. He motivated me, not by encouraging me or telling me he had faith in me, but by stirring me up. He also implied that I might be a quitter and that was just the challenge I needed in that moment to draw another burst of energy out of my own fear and frustration.

  You may not always literally have a coach on your side, or even a mentor that you know, but you can find coaches and mentors in books, videos and audios. Don't forget that; you can carry their words with you in your mind.

- **Other people's belief in you:** Even when you don't believe in yourself, other people's belief in you can fill that void. I was literally riding on the fumes of those kids' belief in me to keep moving forward. As Les Brown told me years ago, "Sometimes you must believe in *somebody else's* belief in you until *your* belief in you kicks in."

Friends, in that five hours and ten minutes, I was *Scared Great*. I had no belief in myself. I was terrified and felt like I was going to die. But I finished that marathon. I achieved what I truly thought was an impossible goal, and not because 'I believed in myself' or because 'I conquered my fear.'

I achieved that day because I *prepared* myself and *Steered my Fear.*

Your Fear Is What Makes You Great

A while back, I joined my daughter to watch an episode of World of Dance, hosted by the brilliant Jennifer Lopez. During this episode, I found myself relating to one particular contestant who was struggling to go onstage. She was a very talented young girl who was expected to give a knockout performance. Just before she was supposed to go out, she was gripped by fear and paralyzed by a lack of confidence. She was visibly upset and said she couldn't go on.

When Jennifer Lopez went backstage to talk to her, the young girl confided that she was too upset to perform because of what was going on in her home life. It was obvious she was worried about exposing the struggles within her family, and ashamed of even talking about the problems on national television. She couldn't bring herself to dance.

This girl's fear and lack of belief in herself brought me right back to the *scared* place of my own childhood. When she broke down crying and said she couldn't go onstage because she felt ashamed of her personal problems and the struggles at home, I knew what she meant.

J-Lo looked at this young girl very closely. When one might have expected her to say something that was just comforting or encouraging, she gave her a powerful piece of advice instead. She said, "Use that feeling. Put it into your dancing."

J-lo explained that all great artists *use* the pain and fear they feel. They don't run from it; they channel it. Their *scared* is what makes them great.

That night the girl steered her fear into her Greatness with a show stopping performance. Did this young girl have to believe in herself? No. Did she have to conquer her fear? No. What she had to do was guide and direct it. She didn't have to overcome it. She didn't have to leave it behind. She had to *steer* it in order to step into her Greatness as a dancer.

It's the same for all of us. The fear that comes up around anything that matters, the hesitation, the question, "What if I fail?" that tries to hold you back...that fear is your friend, not your enemy. Your fear is what makes you great.

Brace Yourself
Tools for Greatness
Tool #7: In a 'Scared Great Moment'

In the moment, how do you channel your fear toward your *Greatness*?

STEP 1. Ask yourself - What am I afraid of?
Assess your feelings. Take a look at them and don't shy away. Pinpoint as clearly as possible what you are afraid of in this moment. If possible, write it down. Don't judge yourself; just let it flow.

Examples:
I'm afraid people will laugh at me.
I'm afraid I'll get rejected.
I'm afraid this investment won't pay off.
I'm afraid I will embarrass myself.

I'm afraid I won't be able to finish the project on my own.
I'm afraid I won't get the job / the promotion/the contract --
whatever it may be.
I'm afraid I'm not enough. I'm afraid I can't do it.

Assess the core feeling, the center-piece of the feeling. How many people right now are sitting on their dreams because they haven't taken the time to assess *what they are even afraid of?* Ask yourself, what *exactly* am I afraid of? Then you can move on to the next step.

STEP 2. Ask yourself - What experience have I had in the past where I felt a similar or greater amount of fear and overcame it?
Put your fear into perspective. If you're worried about not doing well in a job interview and your fear is overwhelming you, ask yourself, what have *I already* overcome in my life? Know that, whatever you're scared of right now, you have probably already been through something worse and overcome it! That's why you're reading this;

174

you're *here*. You have already overcome moments of fear and you can overcome this one, too.

If I'm feeling fear before getting on stage, meeting with someone, or even making a phone call, I think back to one of the *Scared* moments I had as a kid and know that, if I overcame that, I can overcome this too.

STEP 3. Ask yourself - What *CAN* you prepare for?
Not everything is under our control. We can't control other people's feelings, decisions or reactions. We have to accept those in the moment. But there is always *something* we can prepare for. Ask yourself, what *CAN* I do to prepare? Write those things down.

Examples:
If I'm afraid of failing an exam, I can make a study schedule. I can get help from a tutor.
If I'm afraid of doing badly in a job interview, I can prepare a list of potential questions and maybe I

can get a friend to help me practice the interview.

If I'm afraid of making a career change, I can research others who have made similar career changes. I can start reading books and listening to podcasts about the new career I'm interested in. I can attend a workshop or seminar. I can make a list of the individual steps that it will take for me to transition into this new career. I can update my resume.

STEP 4. Ask yourself- What is the *first* step?

You don't have to know every single step it will take to reach your goal in order to take the *first* step. In a *Scared Great Moment*, you don't need to see into the future. You just need to take *one* step.

As I mentioned in a previous chapter, in his book, *Outliers*, Malcolm Gladwell uses the Beatles as an example. They became a great rock band eventually, one of the most famous bands of all time; I didn't happen overnight, but through a long series of next steps, one after the other. Gladwell estimates it took John, Paul, George and Ringo 10,000 hours of practice before they became the Beatles. But they each had to take a first step to get there.

Sometime or other, John had to pick up a guitar and learn a single chord. Ringo had to pick up a pair of drumsticks.

What is your first step?

STEP 5. Ask yourself - *How* can I take that step?
Decide on a specific action and then
  follow through.
Put the letter in the mail.
Send the email.
Go for a walk around the block.
Make the phone call.
Sign up for the class.
Step out the door.

You don't have to know or see or prepare for *every* step -- just take that first one.

CHAPTER TWELVE: IT'S A WRAP

Imagine walking up to complete strangers all day, asking annoyed and busy people to listen to you for just one second so you can tell them about a simple but powerful idea. Imagine getting rejected over and over, as people push past and tell you, 'Not now, no thanks.' Imagine all you want to do is give these strangers a gift, just to remind them there is kindness in the world. What would motivate you to approach one stranger after another with this simple request, when so many don't want to stop and listen?

One of my personal heroes is a young girl named Leah Nelson, and that's just what she has been doing for the last few years. She started her *kindness initiative* when she was in the third grade. She's now a teenager and the founder of a nonprofit organization that is active on multiple continents.

Leah first approached me with one of her handmade woven bracelets at a big community event called Saturday Night Lights in West Sacramento. It's an event designed to bring teachers, families, children, police officers and other members of the community together. I was there with my partner Susan, aka Coach Kindness. Leah came up to me with one of her handmade bracelets that night and said, "Coach Greatness, I want to give you this. And then I just want you to pass it on to someone else and say something kind when you do."

Susan and I both loved this so much we decided to do an interview with Leah (her first!). Moments after that, a local news station interviewed Leah and 24 hours later the story went viral. A video of her had over 11 million views within a few days. Overnight, Leah had launched a movement based on this simple idea of spreading kindness.

Her bracelets now are included in bags at the Academy Awards. Her nonprofit organization, *BecuzICare11*, has gone national. It has raised many thousands of dollars and has used that money on various acts of kindness -- paying the rent for hurricane victims in Texas, providing school supplies for students affected by flooding in Louisiana and bringing Christmas presents to underprivileged children in West Sacramento, among many other things.

Today, over 100 million people have viewed the story of *BecuzICare11*, and Leah has over 60,000 followers on Facebook. Leah's mission is to use her social media platform to do as much good for other people as she can, and to encourage others to pay the kindness forward even if it's just in the form of a compliment. In Leah's words, "In a world with so many issues, let's show other people they are valued."

In one news segment from the early days of Leah's bracelet project, you can see that some people weren't even nice when she approaches them with her bracelets. Just as you would expect, a lot of people ignored her and walked past quickly as if she were asking them for money. They didn't take the time to hear what she had to say. But Leah never let that slow her roll for a second. She stayed positive. She treated every person like a new opportunity. She didn't get discouraged or at least she didn't show it. She didn't let the fear of other people being rude stop her. She channeled her energy into kindness, over and over, one moment, one bracelet and one person at a time.

Why? Because she has found what she's *passious* about. She goes *toward* that feeling, not away from it. It shapes her life every day and it changes the lives of the people around her for the better. That's Greatness.

Brace Yourself: Get Up, Get Out and GO GET IT!

There's Greatness in you. *Feel it.*
You may be scared. *Expect it.*
You may have NO belief. *Accept it.*
You will always feel fear. *Run with it.*
When your mind goes negative, your mouth goes positive. When you no longer try to avoid fear,

when you don't let your *Scared* discourage you, then it is no longer the enemy. Fear becomes your friend, and it will propel you right into your Greatness. When you direct, channel and steer that fear, your Greatness will rise up.

You don't even have to believe me. I believe it FOR you.

I challenge you right now to think of something in your life that gave you that *passious* feeling-- an idea, a thought, a suggestion you heard; a moment in time when you felt so nervous you wanted to run away, but you also felt thrilled beyond belief because *that thing* you wanted to do mattered so much to you.

Now ask yourself, how could that feeling be directed into just one single step? Just ONE step. Don't even think about the second step. Just the first one.

Get Up...

Get Out...

GO GET IT!

I dare you.

Brace Yourself!

About the Author

Born, raised, and educated in Sacramento, CA, Kevin Bracy, AKA Coach Greatness, is a motivational entertainer, executive producer, creator of the First Steps for Speakers online coaching program, and the author of two youth books, "The Top 10 Tips for Teen Success," "Greatness Leaves Clues" and this recently completed third book, 'Scared Great: Steer Your Fear Towards Greatness'.

Over his 22-year career, Kevin has been privileged to speak to associations, organizations, corporations, educators, administrators as well as millions of students across America. For the past 5 years, he has been actively changing the culture of school campuses with his R.E.A.C.H. One Alliance anti-bullying/character education program.

Kevin's message to "Each One, Reach One" is an enthusiastic reminder to encourage people to reach for their Greatness, reach for their wildest dream, and to intentionally impact another person's life every day with the power of positive words and inclusive action.

Kevin's proudest accomplishments are his 20 year marriage to his college sweetheart, Jessica; having a front row seat to see his daughter, KendraJae, living out her wildest dreams; walking beside his son, Kobe J, as he learns to thrive- not just survive- with chronic illness, and to continue to share a message of perseverance and hope to others; while never forgetting Kaleb Julius Bracy who made an indelible mark on the world in his 1 hour and 16 minutes on this earth in 2005.

As a premier anti-bullying speaker in the school district he grew up in, and the voice of the motivational radio segment, "Minute To Win It!" in his hometown, Kevin has made it his mission to "dream globally, but focus locally." These days he invests his time between his family, his community, teaching a "sold out" spin class every Friday and Saturday, and speaking several times a week to audiences ages 4 to 80.

Kevin continues to encourage, inspire and motivate us all to be the greatest version of ourselves and to positively #EachOneReachOne every day.